COLLAPSIBLE BASKET PATTERNS

Rick and Karen Longabaugh

THE BERRY BASKET

Dedication

We dedicate this book to our two sons, James and Cameron, and to our families for all the unending faith and support they have shown us.

Acknowledgements / Credits

Pattern Designs

Rick Longabaugh
Ardis Longabaugh
Tana Althauser
Lorna Smith

Graphic Design

Lorna Smith Graphic Design
Chehalis, Washington

Photography

Greg Krogstad Photography
Seattle, Washington

ISBN 0-9633112-0-4

Contents

Instructions

Introduction

All patterns in this book can be cut on either the bandsaw or scrollsaw. See page 5 for specific bandsaw instructions and page 6 for specific scrollsaw intructions.

Materials

Saw Blades
   Bandsaw - 1/8" Standard gauge blade (.020 thickness)
   Scrollsaw - #9 blade
3/4 " Hardwood: ash, walnut, mahogany, cherry, maple, oak, etc.
Clamps
Double - sided tape or spray adhesive

6/32 Machine screws
   Flathead ▷▨▨▨▨▨▨▨ or
   Roundhead ⊂▨▨▨▨▨▨▨
Small drum or pad sander
Oil (Danish, Tung or Min-Wax)
1/8" Drill bit
Wood glue

General Instructions

To use this pattern book most effectively, we suggest making photo copies of the patterns you wish to cut out. An advantage to the copier is that you can enlarge or reduce the pattern to fit the size wood you choose to use. Use double-sided tape or a spray adhesive to adhere the pattern to the wood. Spray adhesives can be purchased at most arts & crafts, photography, and department stores. Pay special attention to purchase one that states "temporary bond" or "repositionable". Lightly spray the back of the pattern, not the wood, then position the pattern onto the work piece.

Two factors will determine how deep the basket will fold out, the thickness of the blade, and the bevel of the table when cutting. A thicker blade produces a deeper basket, as does the 4° bevel over the 5°. Therefore, we recommend practicing with an inexpensive grade of wood until you determine the proper bevel for the thickness of the blade you are using. In the materials listed above we have recommended blade sizes for the bandsaw and scrollsaw, and have given bevels on each pattern to get you started. **Note:** If you use a bandsaw blade other than the thickness listed above, you may need to put some weight in the basket for a few hours until it will remain open on its own.

We have stated a drill bit size and corresponding machine screw size in the materials listed above. If, however, you choose to use a size other than what is listed, use a drill bit one size smaller than the machine screws you are using. This will ensure that the screws will fit snugly, providing enough resistance so the basket does not swing freely. You can determine the length of the machine screw you need for any given pivot point by measuring the length of its dotted line on the pattern. If you wish to counter sink the screw, keep in mind that you will need a shorter length of screw than what the dotted line measured.

Sand any rough edges on the outer shape and the first rung of the basket. If the basket or foot catches on any edges when pivoted, try sanding a little more. For a more refined look use a roundover router bit on the edges.

When the basket is completed, soak it in oil according to the manufactures' instructions.

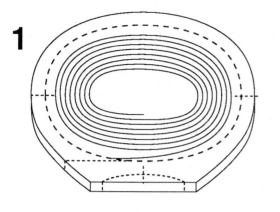

1

Bandsaw Instructions

Step 1 Adhere pattern to work piece. Cut outer shape of basket.

Step 2 Mark the drill points using a hammer and center punch. Drill basket and foot pivot points the length of their dotted lines.

Step 3 Cut along dashed lines (with table flat) to separate inner basket and foot. Glue outer shape where cut was made, and clamp.

Step 4 Using the bevel indicated on the pattern, cut basket rungs following the solid line, shut off saw and back out blade. Glue 1"-2" at start of cut, and clamp.

Step 5 Assemble basket and foot with screws at drilled pivot points.

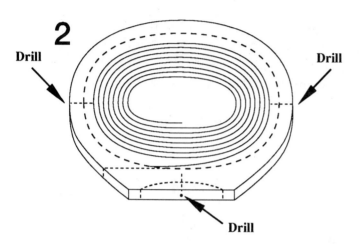

2

Drill

Drill

Drill

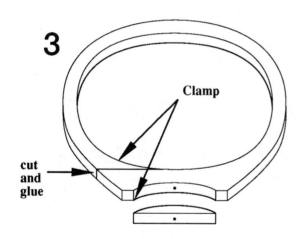

3

Clamp

cut
and
glue

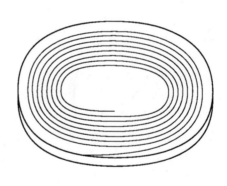

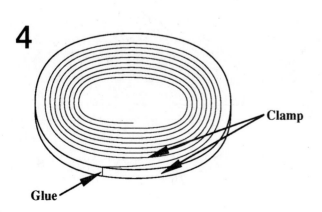

4

Clamp

Glue

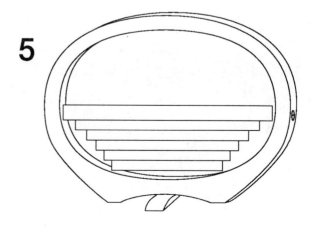

5

1

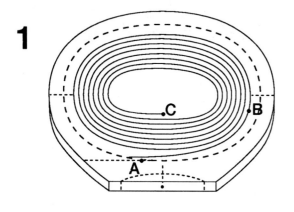

Scrollsaw Instructions

Step 1 Adhere pattern to work piece. Cut outer shape of basket.

Step 2 Mark the drill points using a hammer and center punch. Drill basket and foot pivot points the length of their dotted lines.

2

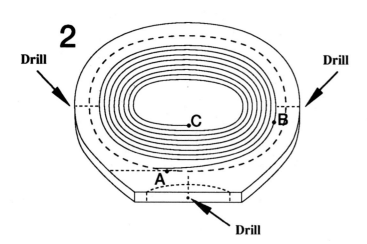

Drill

Drill

Drill

Step 3 With table flat, cut along dashed lines to separate foot. Drill at points A, B, C using a 1/16" drill bit. Beginning at Point A, cut along dashed lines (with table flat) to separate inner basket from the outer shape.

Step 4 Using the bevel indicated on the pattern, cut basket rungs following the solid line. If your table tilts to the left begin your cut at Point C and finish at Point B. If your table tilts to the right begin your cut at Point B and finish at Point C. **Note**: It is easier to begin at Point C and end at Point B.

Step 5 Assemble basket and foot with screws at drilled pivot points.

3

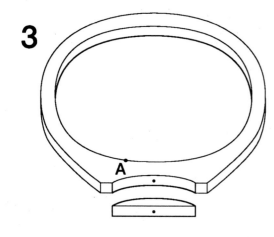

4

5

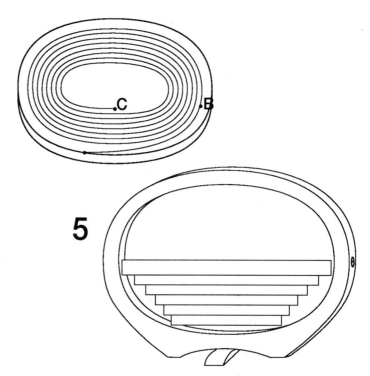

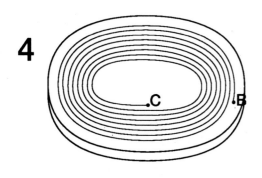

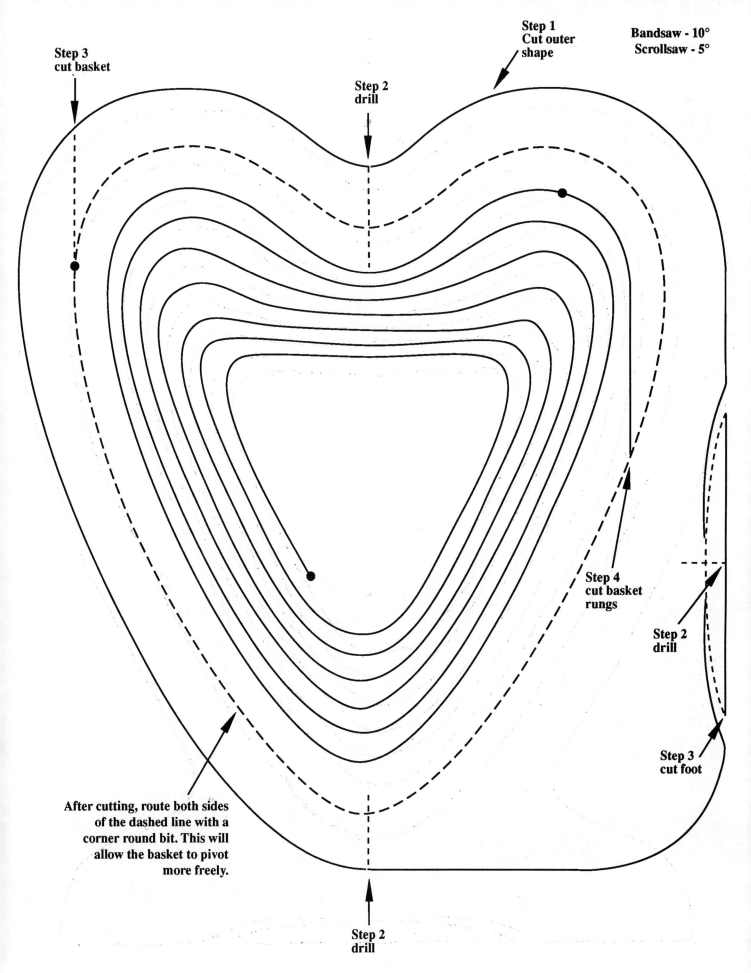

Step 3
cut basket

Step 2
drill

Step 1
Cut outer
shape

Bandsaw - 10°
Scrollsaw - 5°

Step 4
cut basket
rungs

Step 2
drill

Step 3
cut foot

After cutting, route both sides
of the dashed line with a
corner round bit. This will
allow the basket to pivot
more freely.

Step 2
drill

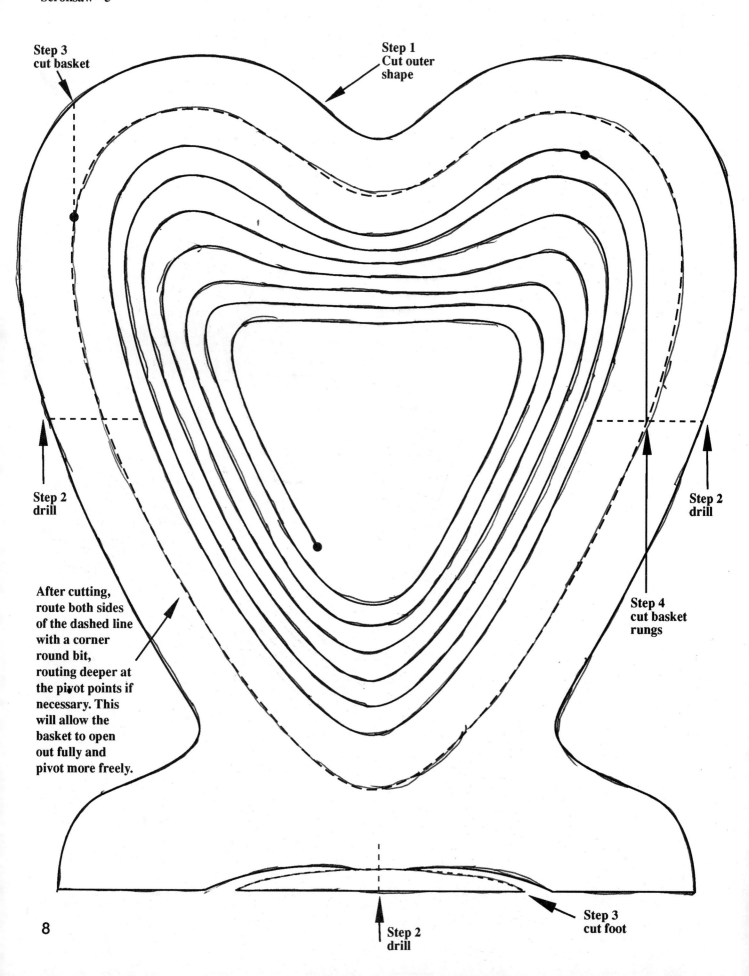

Bandsaw - 10°
Scrollsaw - 5°

Step 3
cut basket

Step 1
Cut outer
shape

Step 2
drill

After cutting,
route both sides
of the dashed line
with a corner
round bit,
routing deeper at
the pivot points if
necessary. This
will allow the
basket to open
out fully and
pivot more freely.

Step 2
drill

Step 4
cut basket
rungs

8

Step 2
drill

Step 3
cut foot

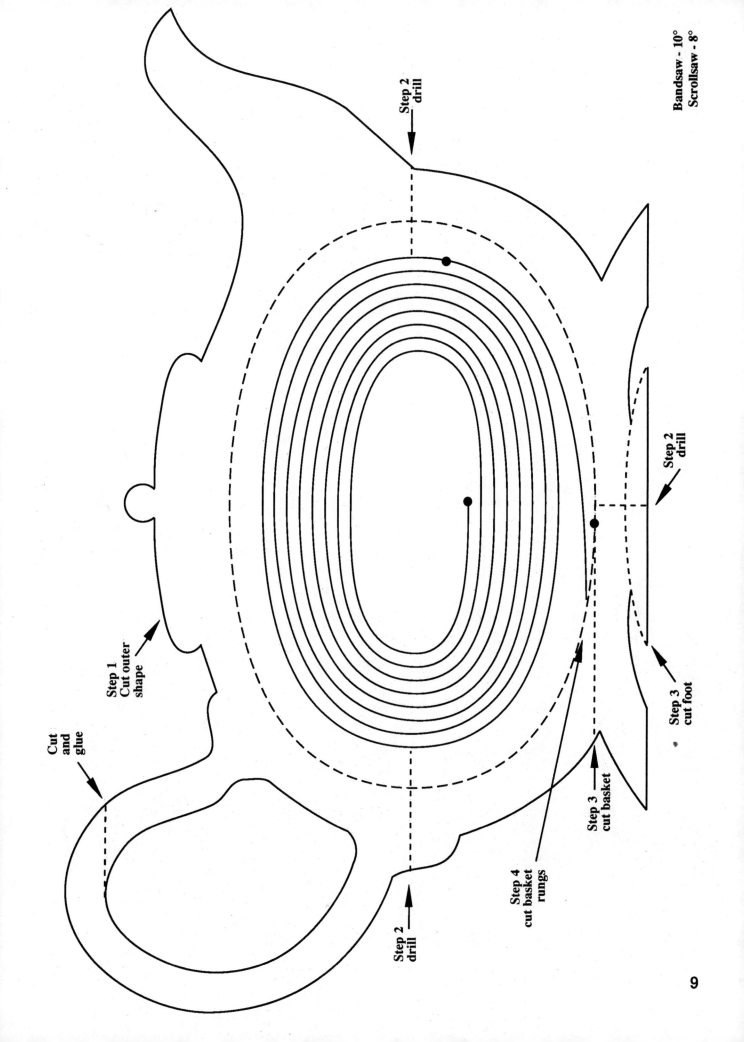

Cut
and
glue

Step 1
Cut outer
shape

Step 2
drill

Step 2
drill

Step 4
cut basket
rungs

Step 3
cut basket

Step 3
cut foot

Step 2
drill

Bandsaw - 10°
Scrollsaw - 8°

9

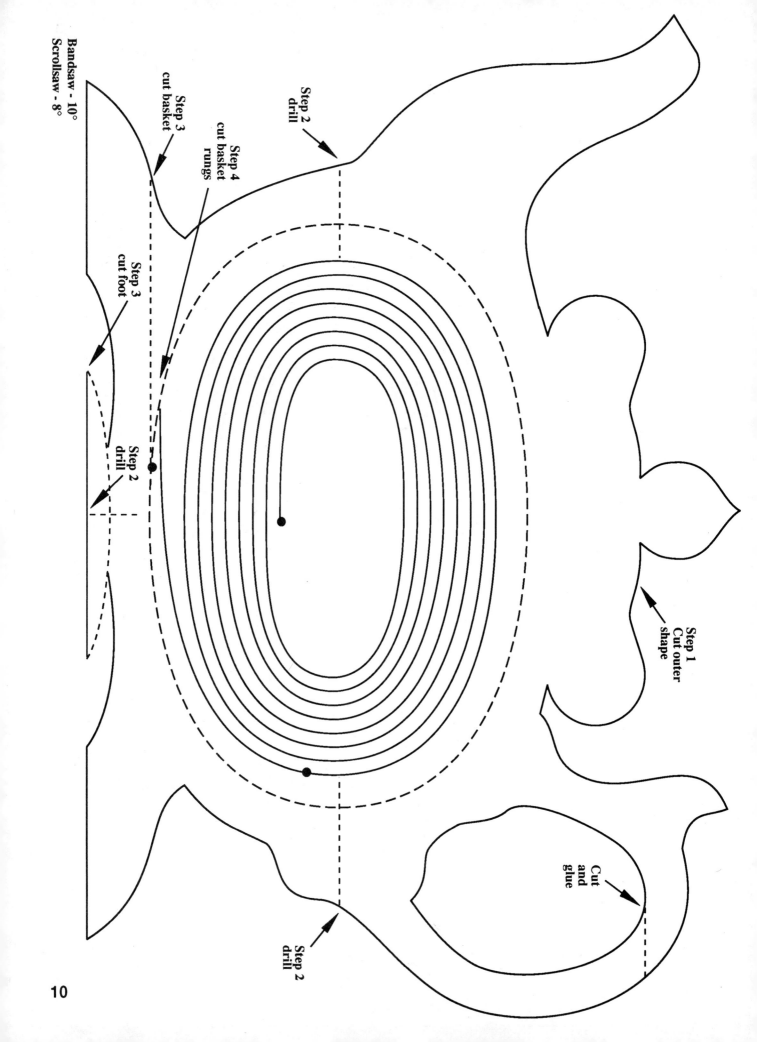

Bandsaw - 10°
Scrollsaw - 8°

Step 3
cut basket

Step 4
cut basket
rungs

Step 2
drill

Step 1
Cut outer
shape

Step 3
cut foot

Step 2
drill

Cut
and
glue

Step 2
drill

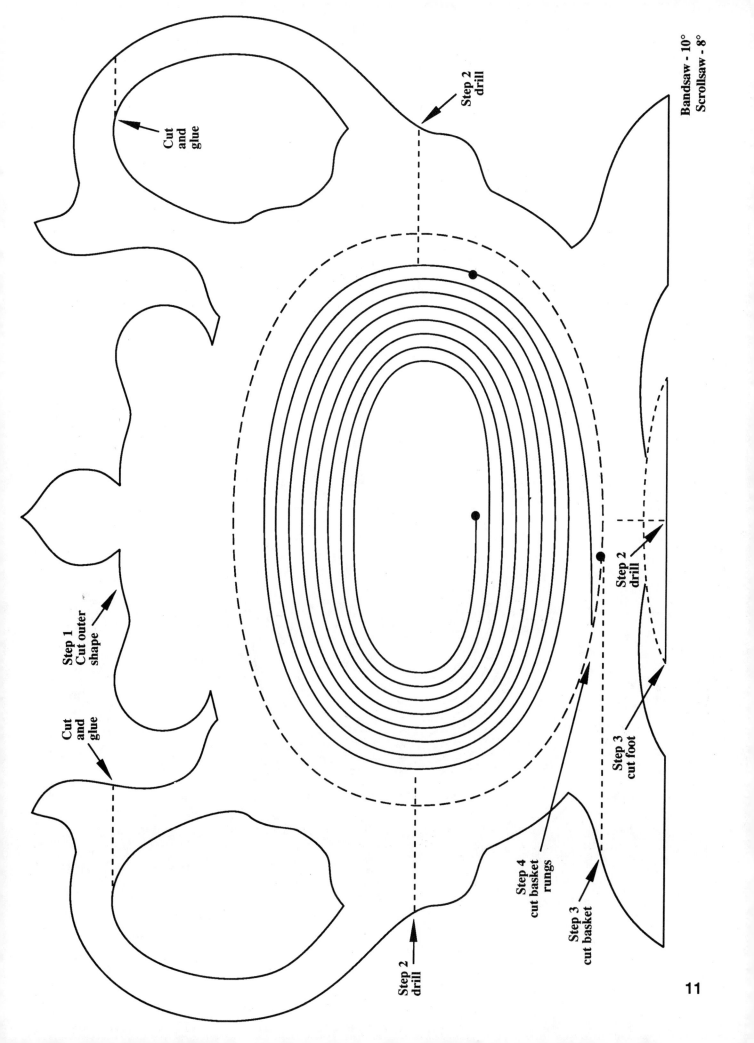

Cut and glue

Step 2 drill

Cut outer shape
Step 1

Cut and glue

Step 2 drill

Step 3 cut foot

Step 3 cut basket

Step 4 cut basket rungs

Step 2 drill

Bandsaw - 10°
Scrollsaw - 8°

11

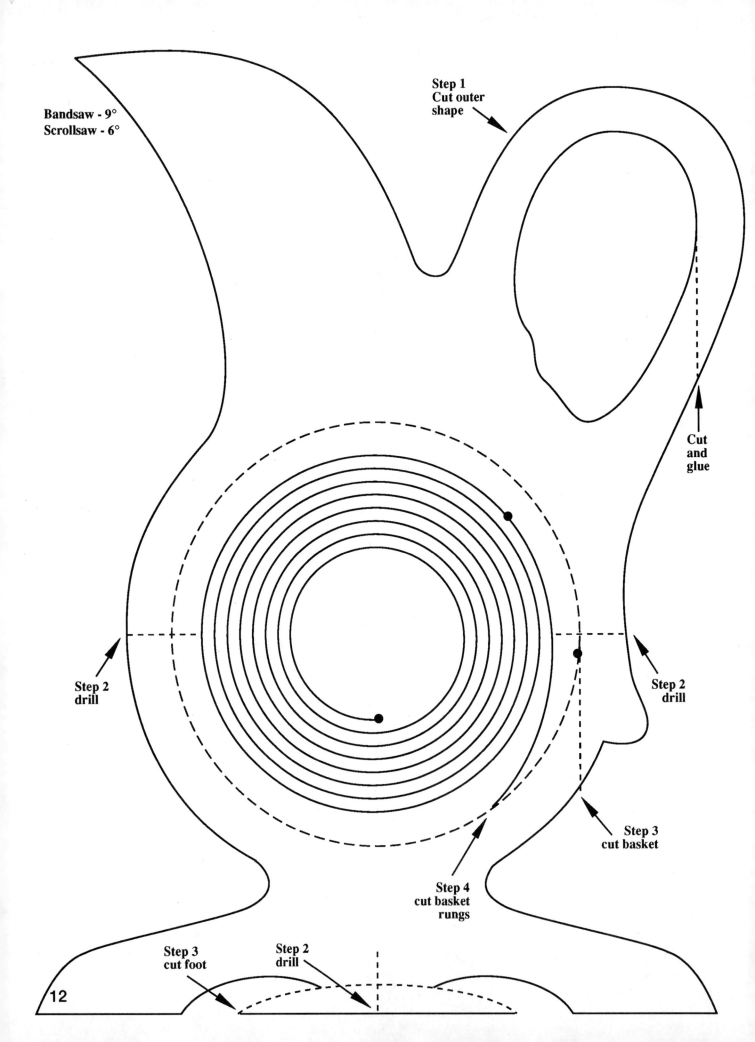

Bandsaw - 9°
Scrollsaw - 6°

Step 1
Cut outer
shape

Cut
and
glue

Step 2
drill

Step 2
drill

Step 3
cut basket

Step 4
cut basket
rungs

Step 3
cut foot

Step 2
drill

12

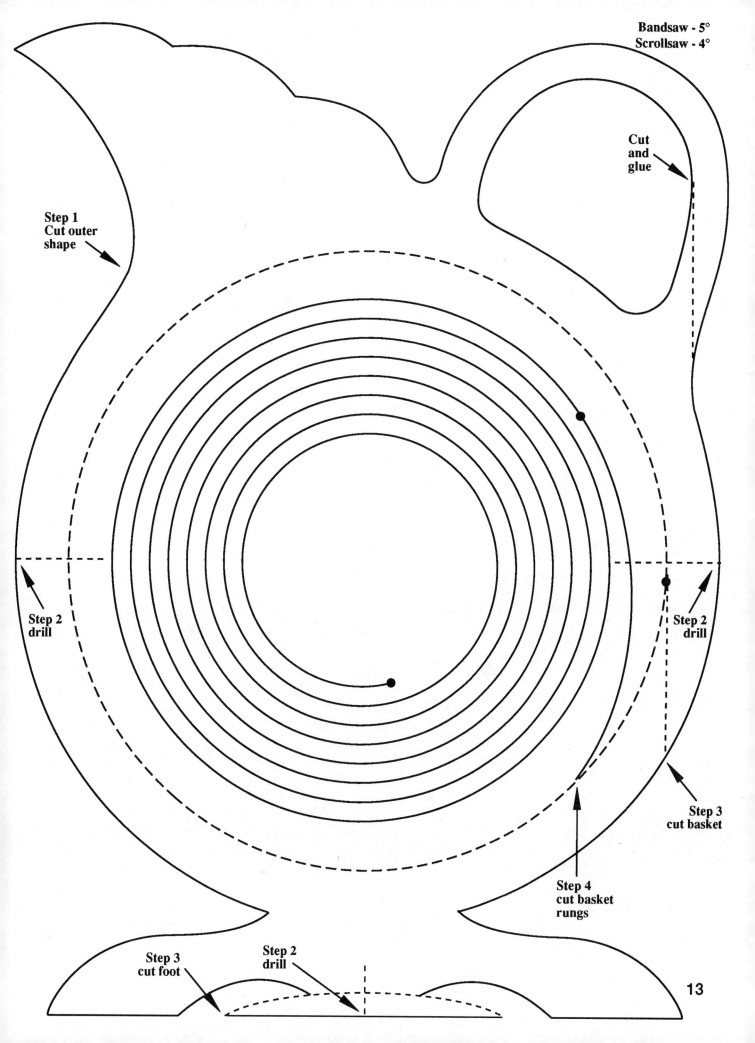

Bandsaw - 5°
Scrollsaw - 4°

Cut
and
glue

Step 1
Cut outer
shape

Step 2
drill

Step 2
drill

Step 3
cut basket

Step 4
cut basket
rungs

Step 3
cut foot

Step 2
drill

13

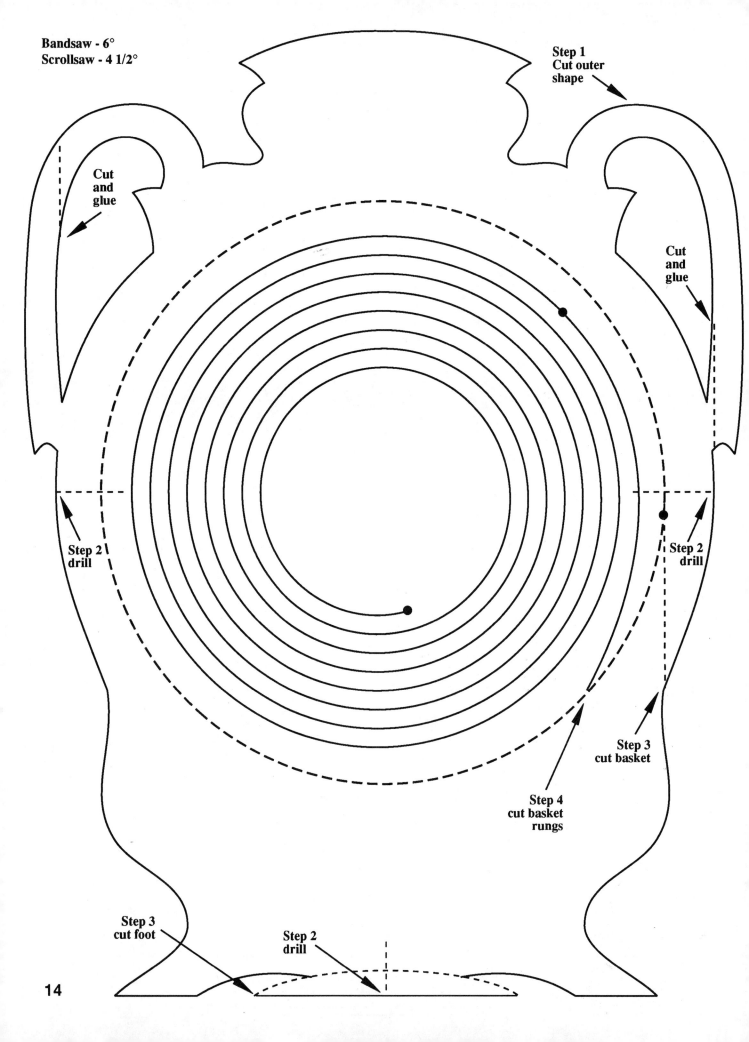

Bandsaw - 6°
Scrollsaw - 4 1/2°

Step 1
Cut outer
shape

Cut
and
glue

Cut
and
glue

Step 2
drill

Step 2
drill

Step 3
cut basket

Step 4
cut basket
rungs

Step 3
cut foot

Step 2
drill

14

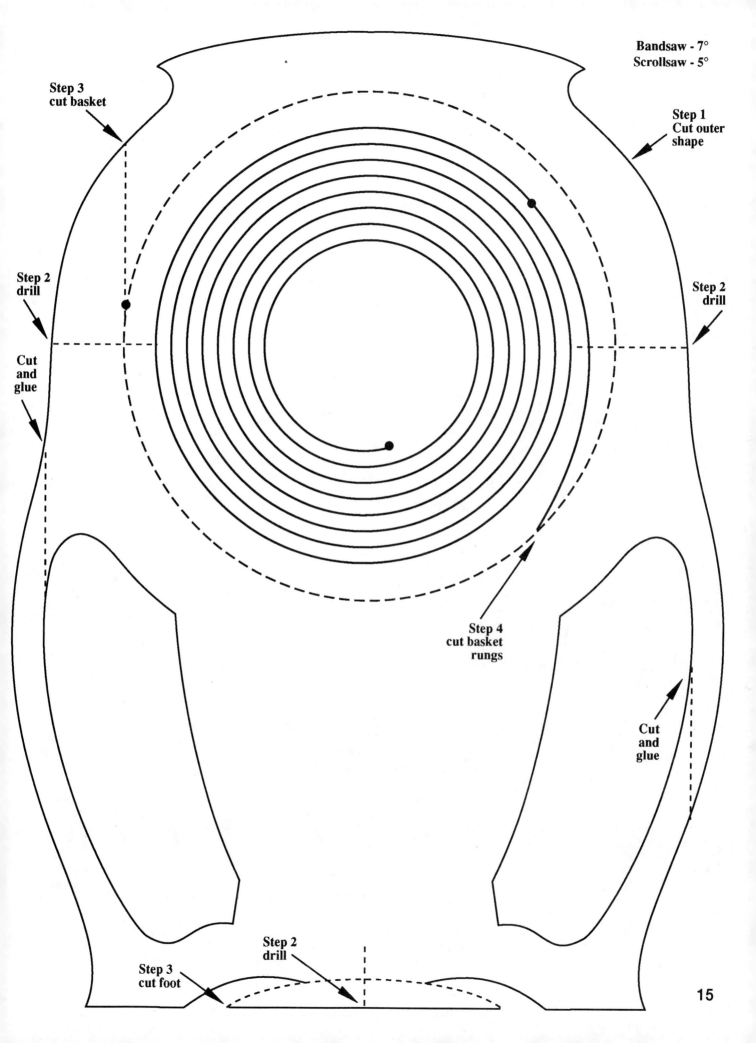

Bandsaw - 7°
Scrollsaw - 5°

Step 3
cut basket

Step 1
Cut outer
shape

Step 2
drill

Step 2
drill

Cut
and
glue

Step 4
cut basket
rungs

Cut
and
glue

Step 2
drill

Step 3
cut foot

15

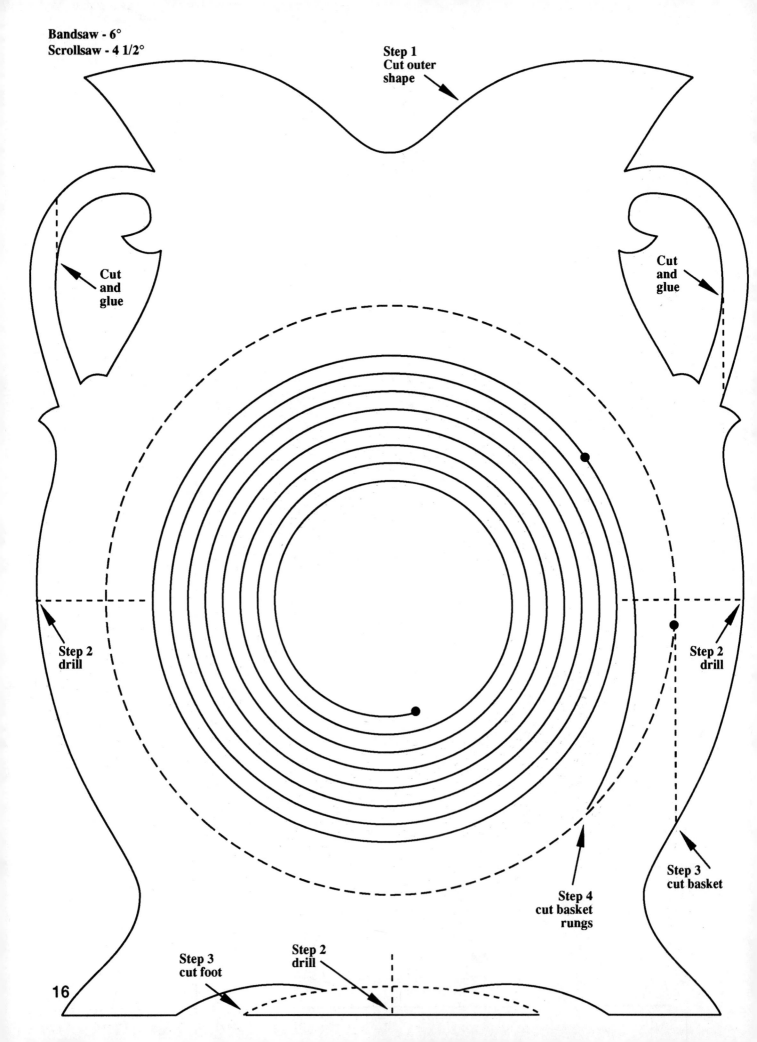

Bandsaw - 6°
Scrollsaw - 4 1/2°

Step 1
Cut outer
shape

Cut
and
glue

Cut
and
glue

Step 2
drill

Step 2
drill

Step 4
cut basket
rungs

Step 3
cut basket

Step 3
cut foot

Step 2
drill

16

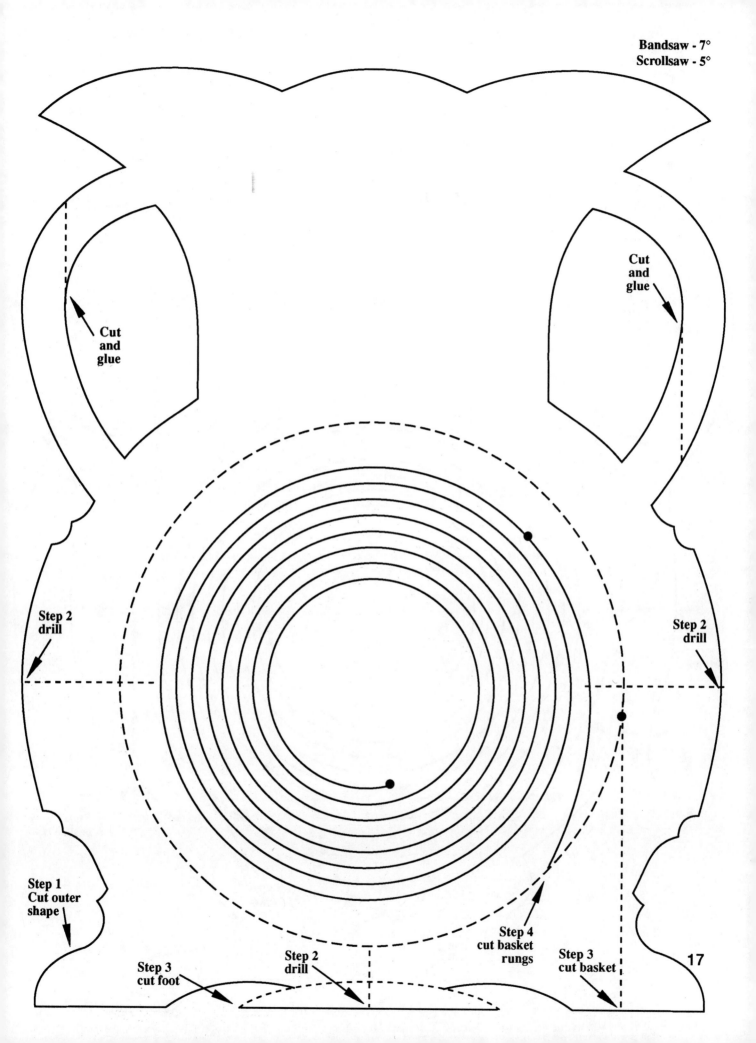

Bandsaw - 7°
Scrollsaw - 5°

Cut
and
glue

Cut
and
glue

Step 2
drill

Step 2
drill

Step 1
Cut outer
shape

Step 4
cut basket
rungs

17

Step 3
cut foot

Step 2
drill

Step 3
cut basket

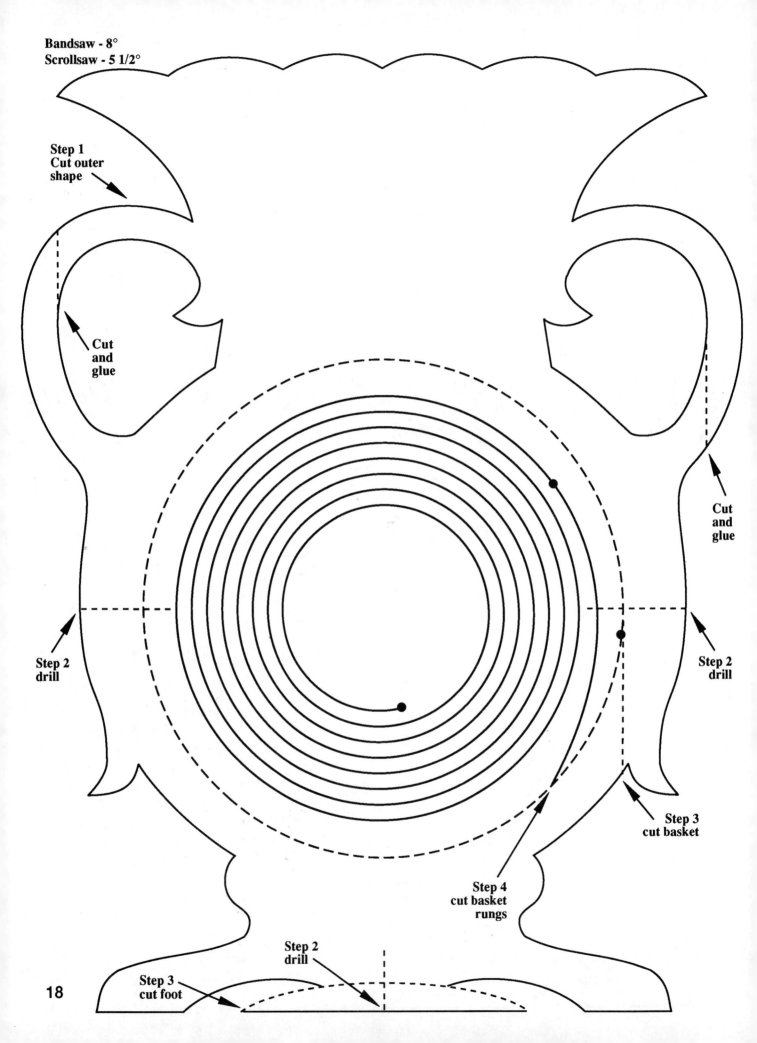

Bandsaw - 8°
Scrollsaw - 5 1/2°

Step 1
Cut outer
shape

Cut
and
glue

Cut
and
glue

Step 2
drill

Step 2
drill

Step 3
cut basket

Step 4
cut basket
rungs

Step 2
drill

Step 3
cut foot

18

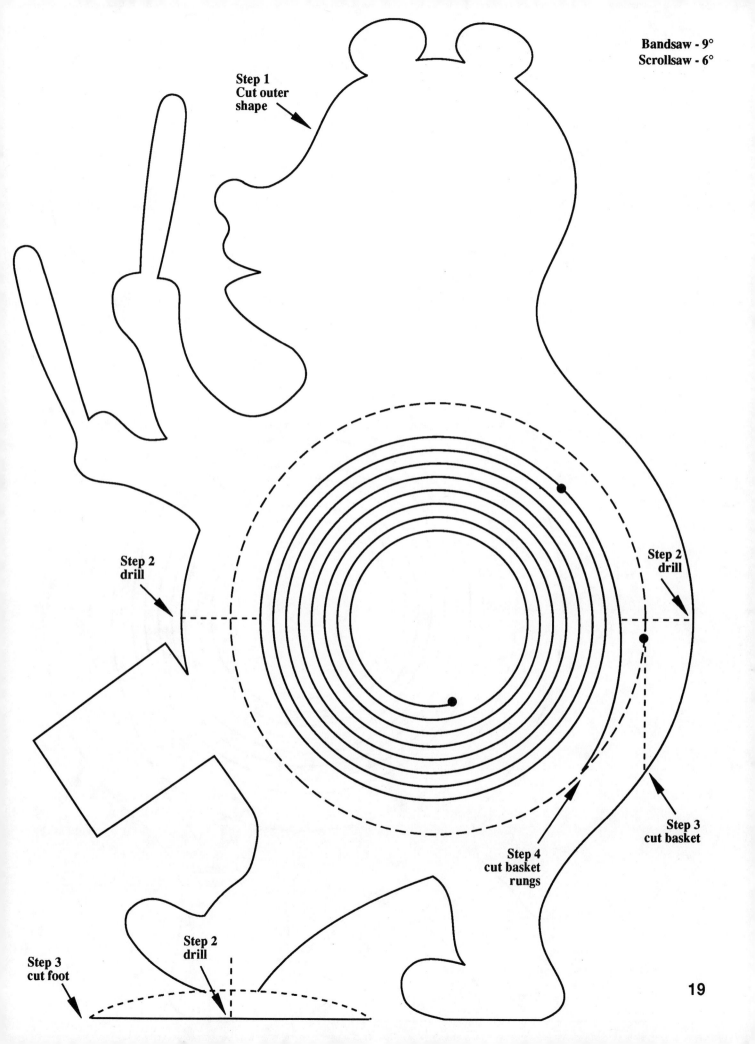

Bandsaw - 9°
Scrollsaw - 6°

Step 1
Cut outer
shape

Step 2
drill

Step 2
drill

Step 4
cut basket
rungs

Step 3
cut basket

Step 2
drill

Step 3
cut foot

19

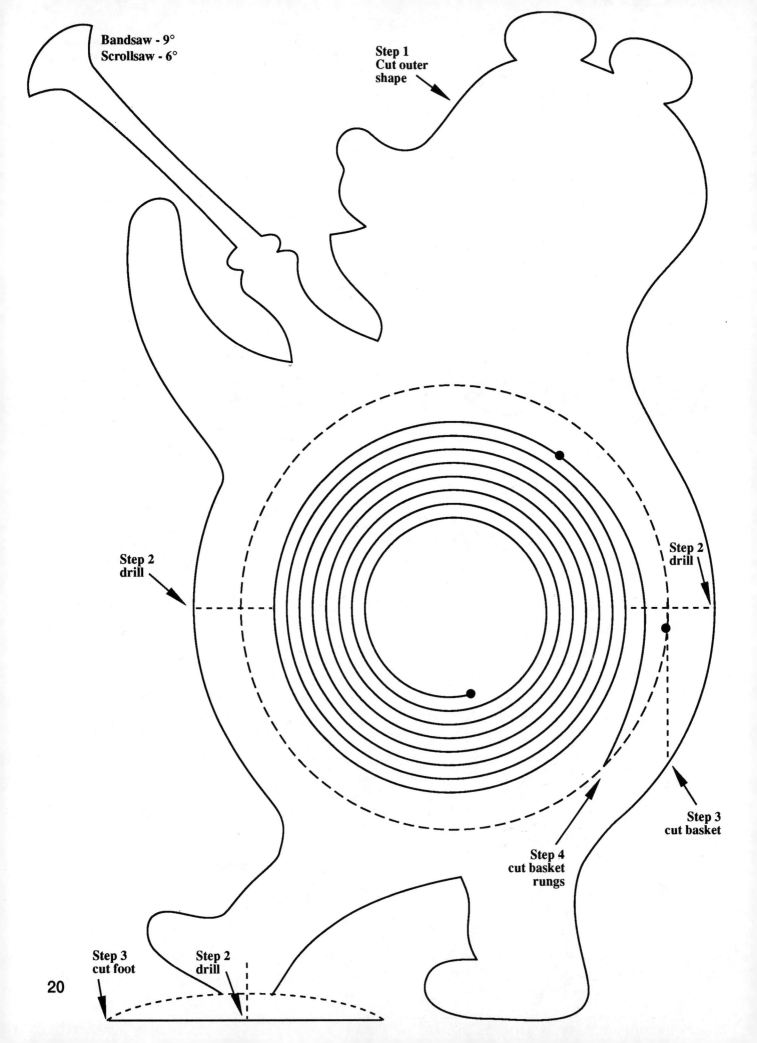

Bandsaw - 9°
Scrollsaw - 6°

Step 1
Cut outer
shape

Step 2
drill

Step 2
drill

Step 2
drill

Step 3
cut basket

Step 4
cut basket
rungs

Step 3
cut foot

Step 2
drill

20

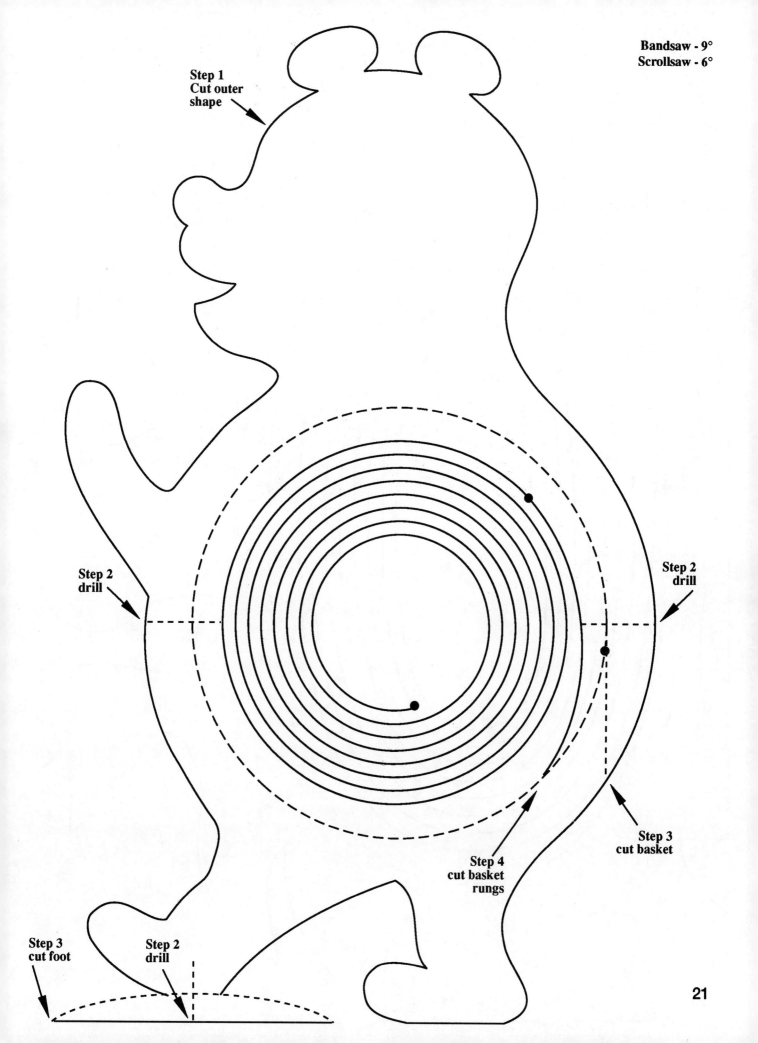

Step 1
Cut outer
shape

Bandsaw - 9°
Scrollsaw - 6°

Step 2
drill

Step 2
drill

Step 4
cut basket
rungs

Step 3
cut basket

Step 3
cut foot

Step 2
drill

21

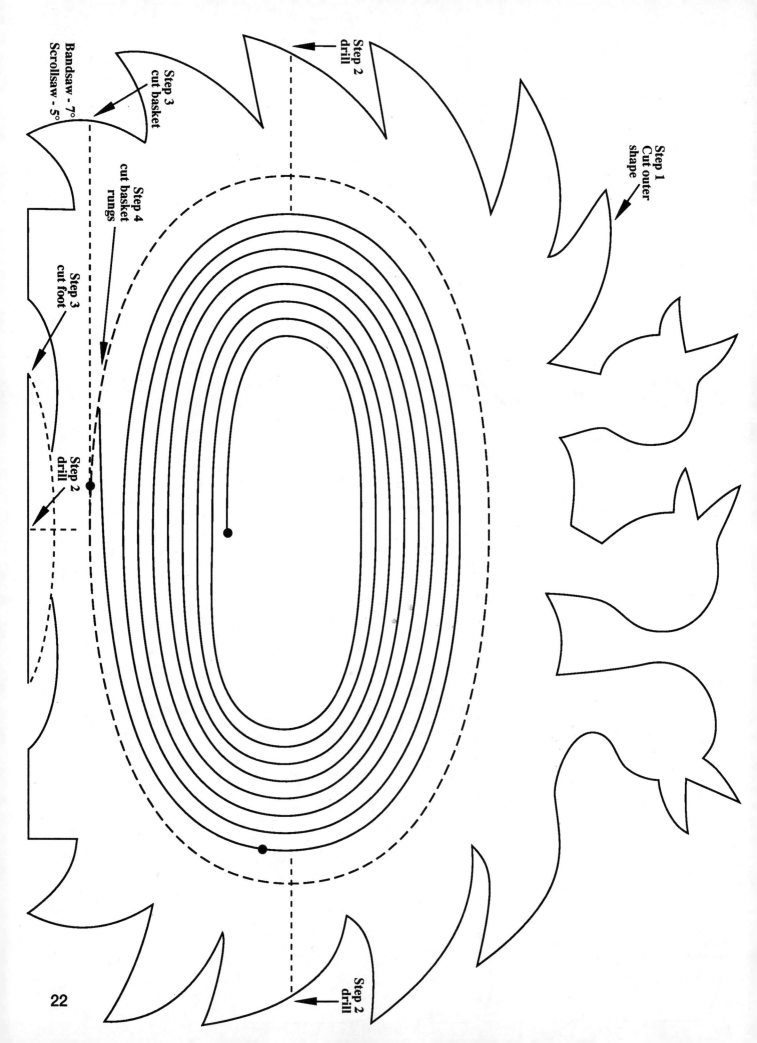

Step 2
drill

Step 1
Cut outer
shape

Step 3
cut basket

Bandsaw - 7°
Scrollsaw - 5°

Step 4
cut basket
rungs

Step 3
cut foot

Step 2
drill

Step 2
drill

22

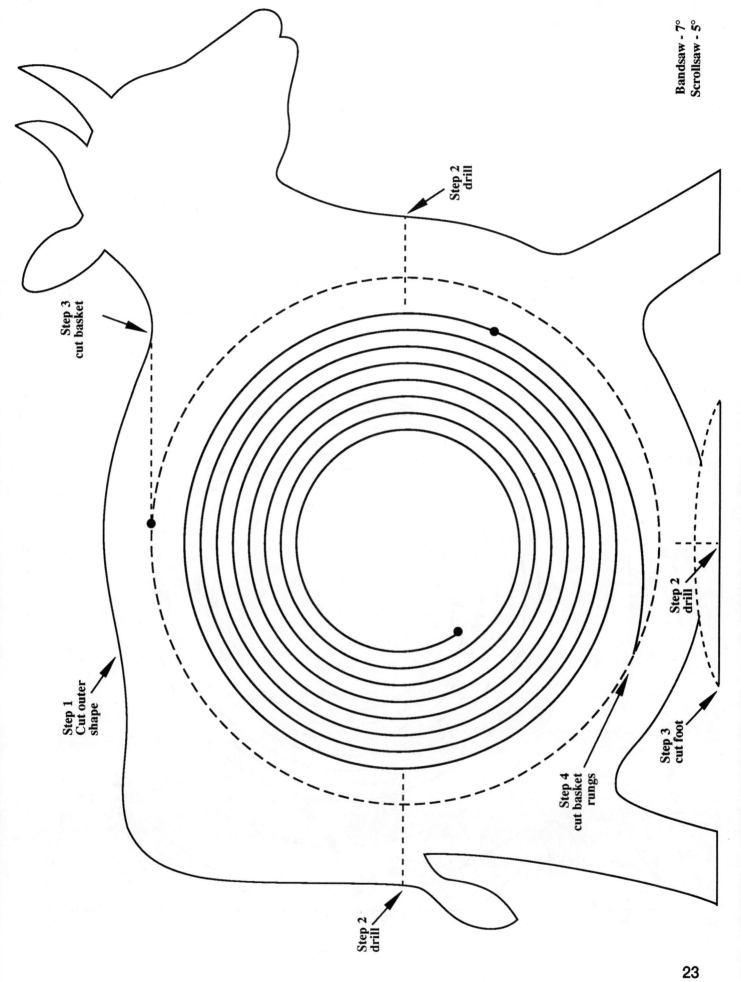

Step 3
cut basket

Step 2
drill

Step 1
Cut outer
shape

Step 2
drill

Step 4
cut basket
rungs

Step 3
cut foot

Step 2
drill

Bandsaw - 7°
Scrollsaw - 5°

23

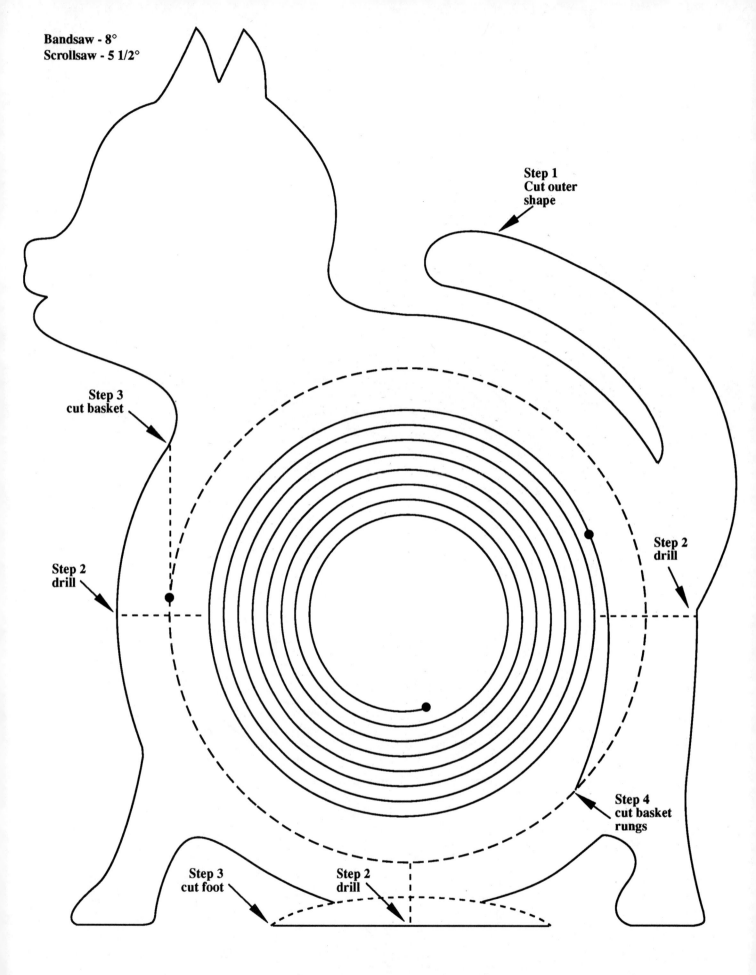

Bandsaw - 8°
Scrollsaw - 5 1/2°

Step 1
Cut outer
shape

Step 3
cut basket

Step 2
drill

Step 2
drill

Step 4
cut basket
rungs

Step 3
cut foot

Step 2
drill

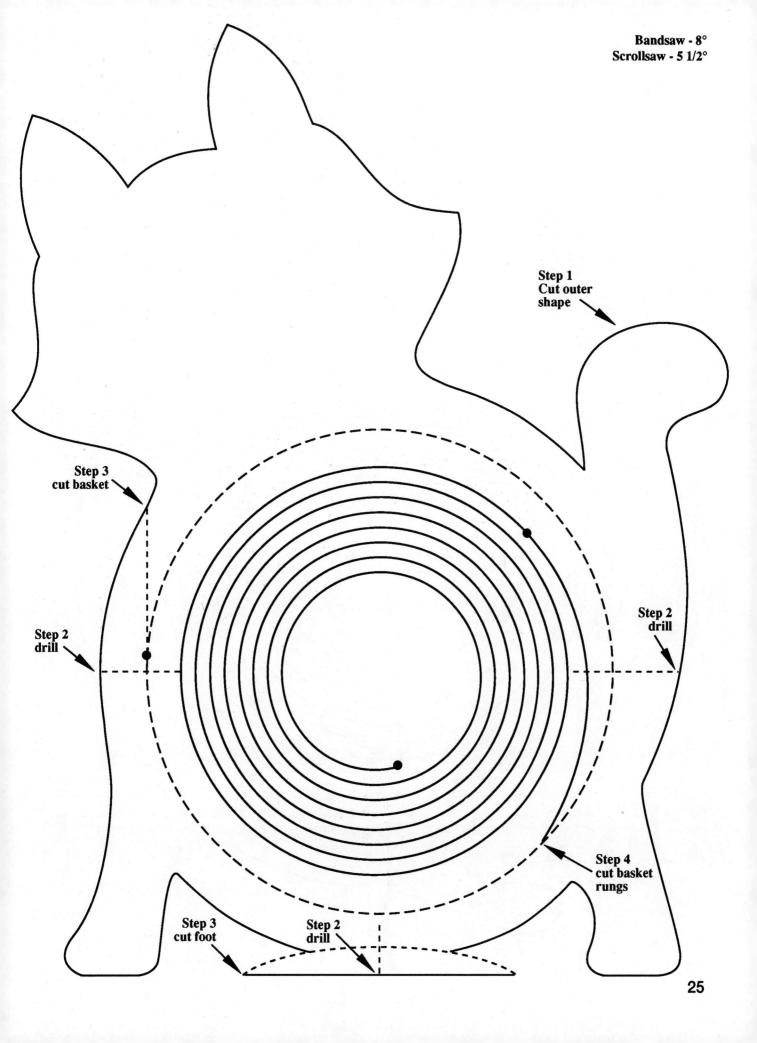

Bandsaw - 8°
Scrollsaw - 5 1/2°

Step 1
Cut outer
shape

Step 3
cut basket

Step 2
drill

Step 2
drill

Step 4
cut basket
rungs

Step 3
cut foot

Step 2
drill

25

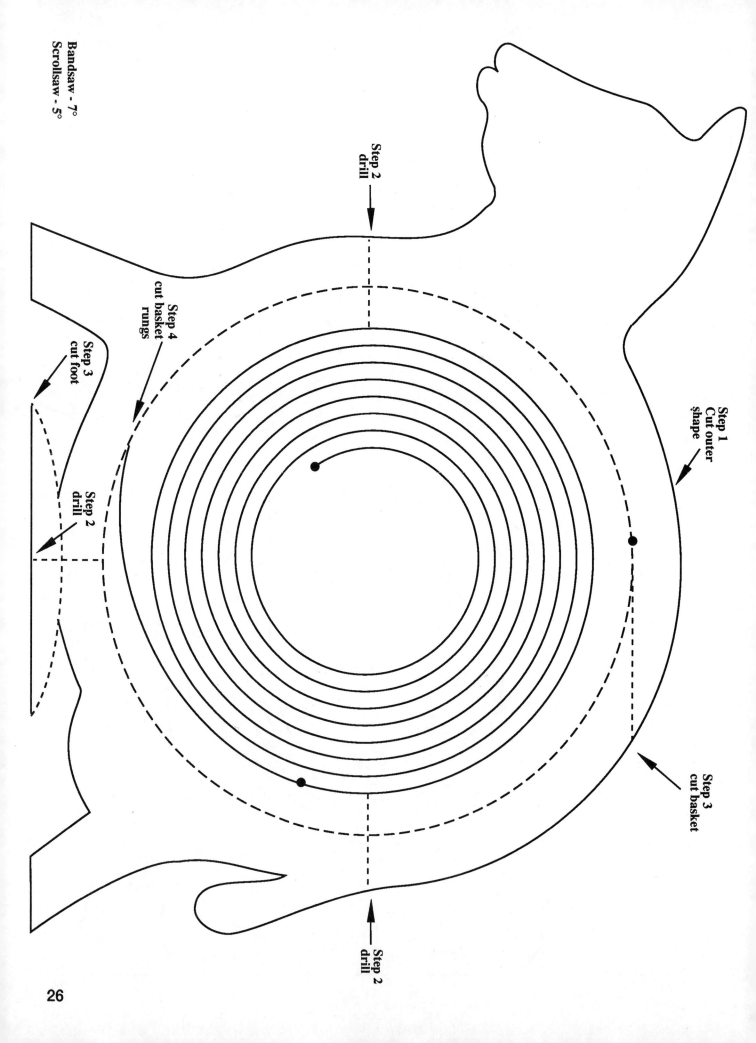

Bandsaw - 7°
Scrollsaw - 5°

Step 2
drill

Step 4
cut basket
rungs

Step 3
cut foot

Step 2
drill

Step 1
Cut outer
shape

Step 3
cut basket

Step 2
drill

26

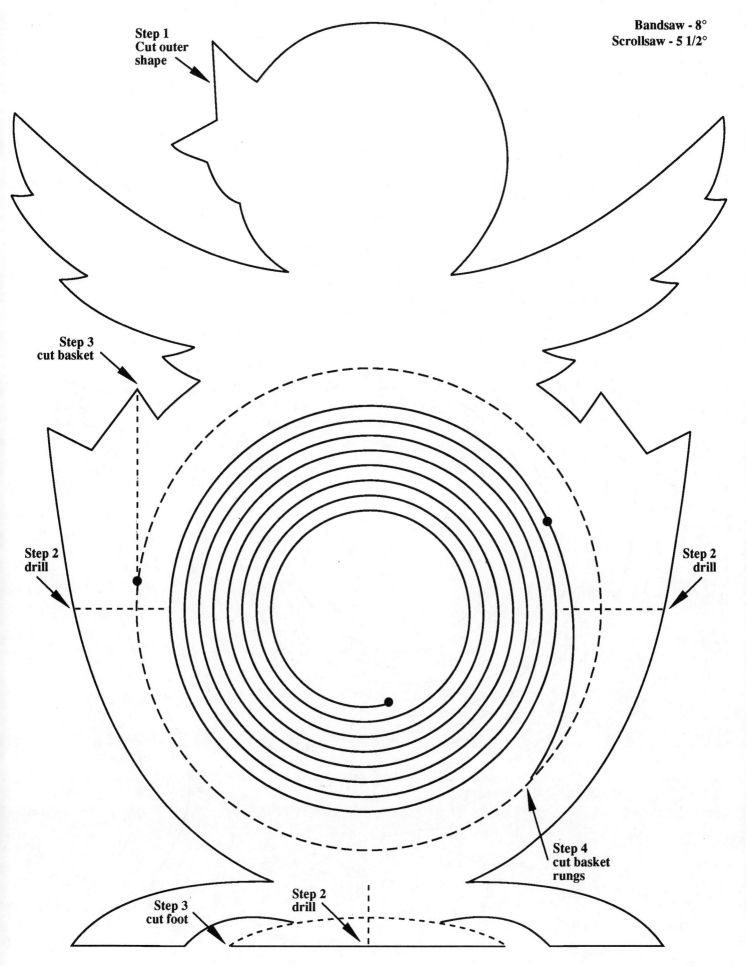

Step 1
Cut outer
shape

Bandsaw - 8°
Scrollsaw - 5 1/2°

Step 3
cut basket

Step 2
drill

Step 2
drill

Step 4
cut basket
rungs

Step 3
cut foot

Step 2
drill

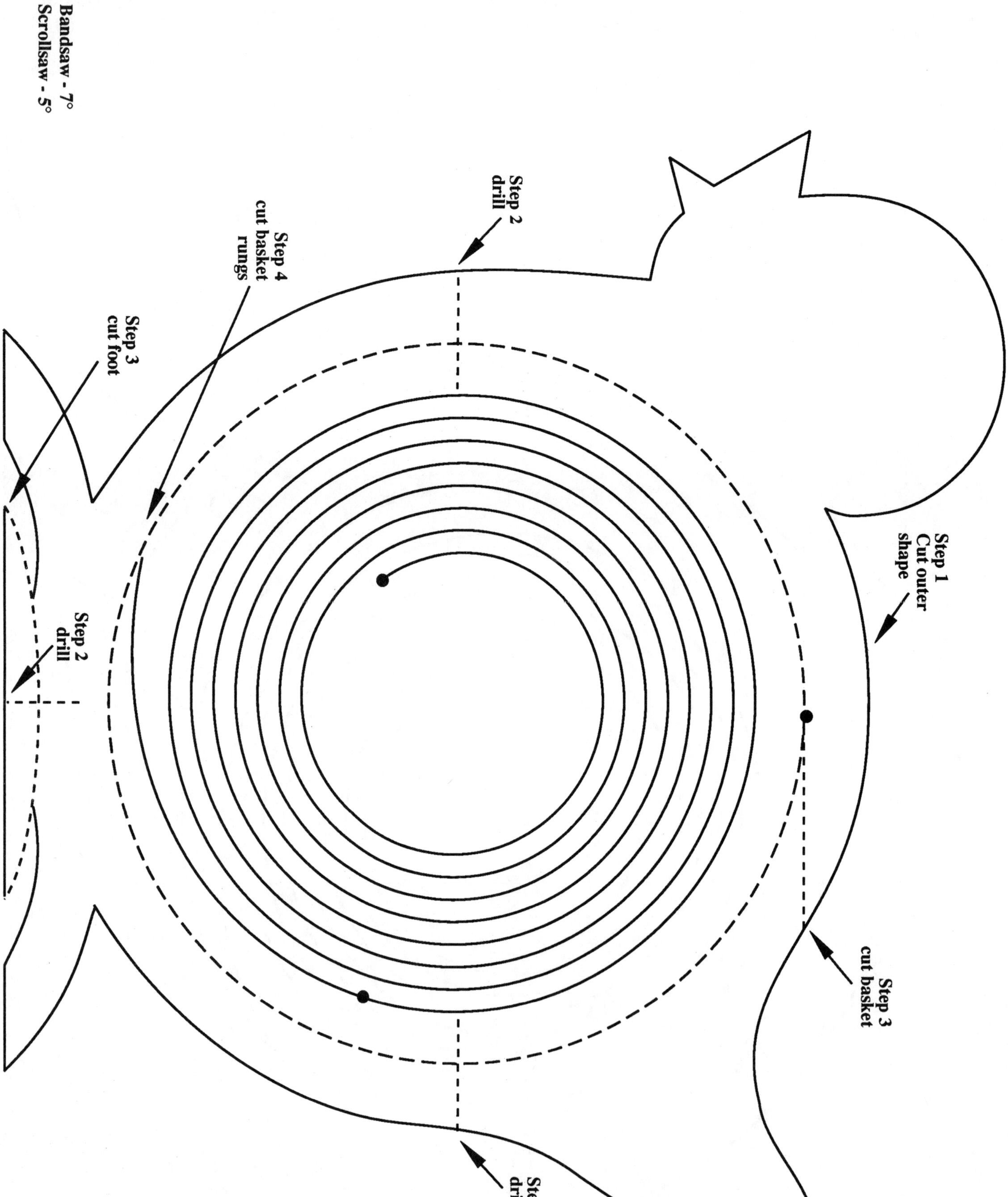

Step 2
drill

Step 4
cut basket
rungs

Step 3
cut foot

Step 2
drill

Step 1
Cut outer
shape

Step 3
cut basket

Step 2
drill

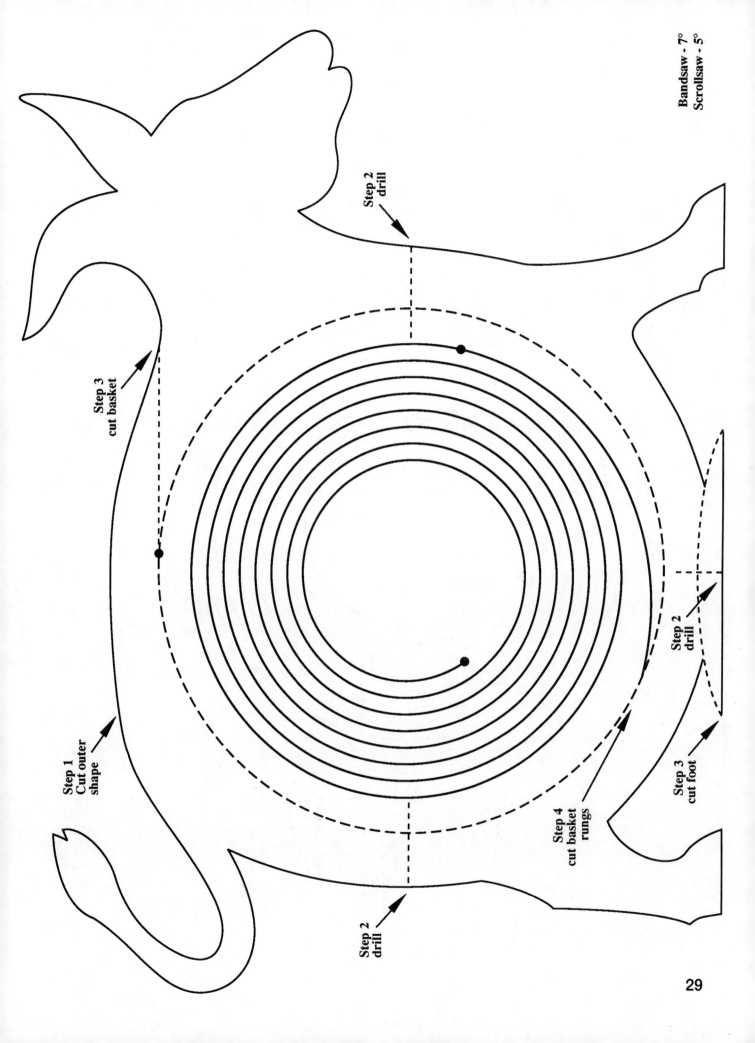

Bandsaw - 7°
Scrollsaw - 5°

Step 2
drill

Step 3
cut basket

Step 1
Cut outer
shape

Step 2
drill

Step 2
drill

Step 3
cut foot

Step 4
cut basket
rungs

29

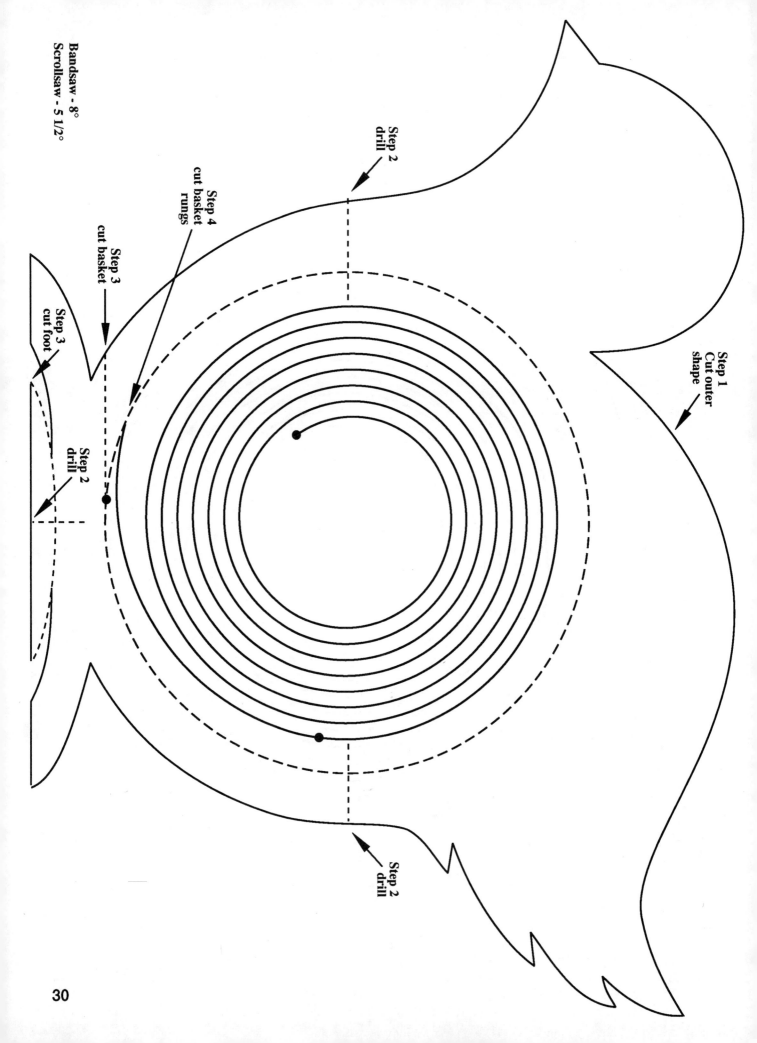

Step 2
drill

Step 4
cut basket
rungs

Step 3
cut basket

Step 3
cut foot

Step 2
drill

Step 1
Cut outer
shape

Step 2
drill

Bandsaw - 8°
Scrollsaw - 5 1/2°

30

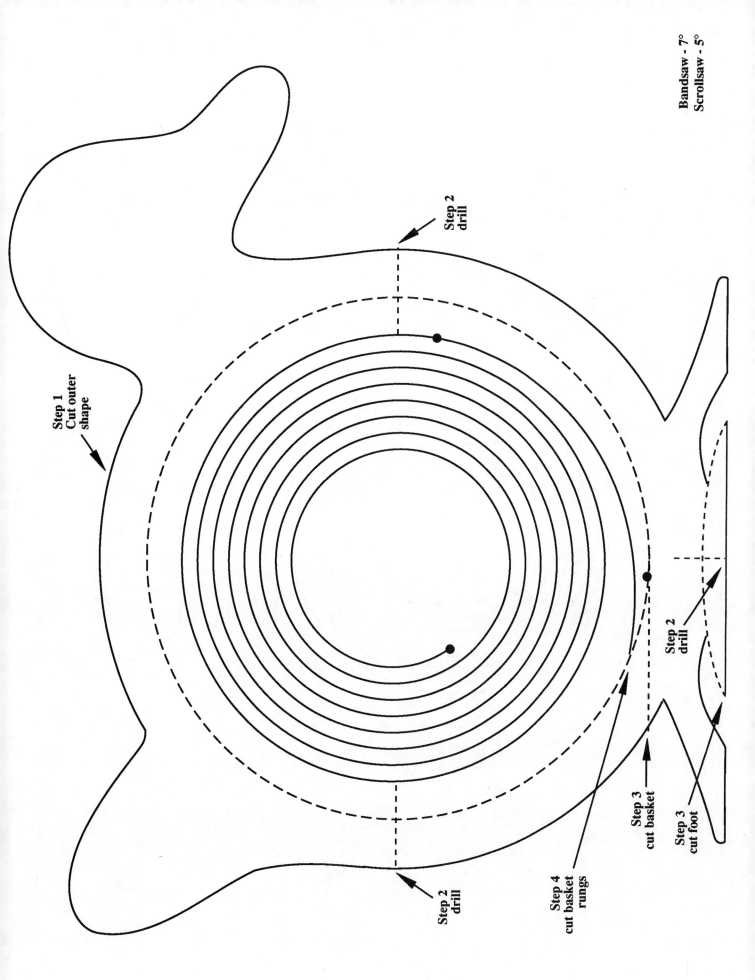

Step 1
Cut outer shape

Step 2
drill

Step 2
drill

Step 2
drill

Step 3
cut basket

Step 3
cut foot

Step 4
cut basket rungs

Bandsaw - 7°
Scrollsaw - 5°

31

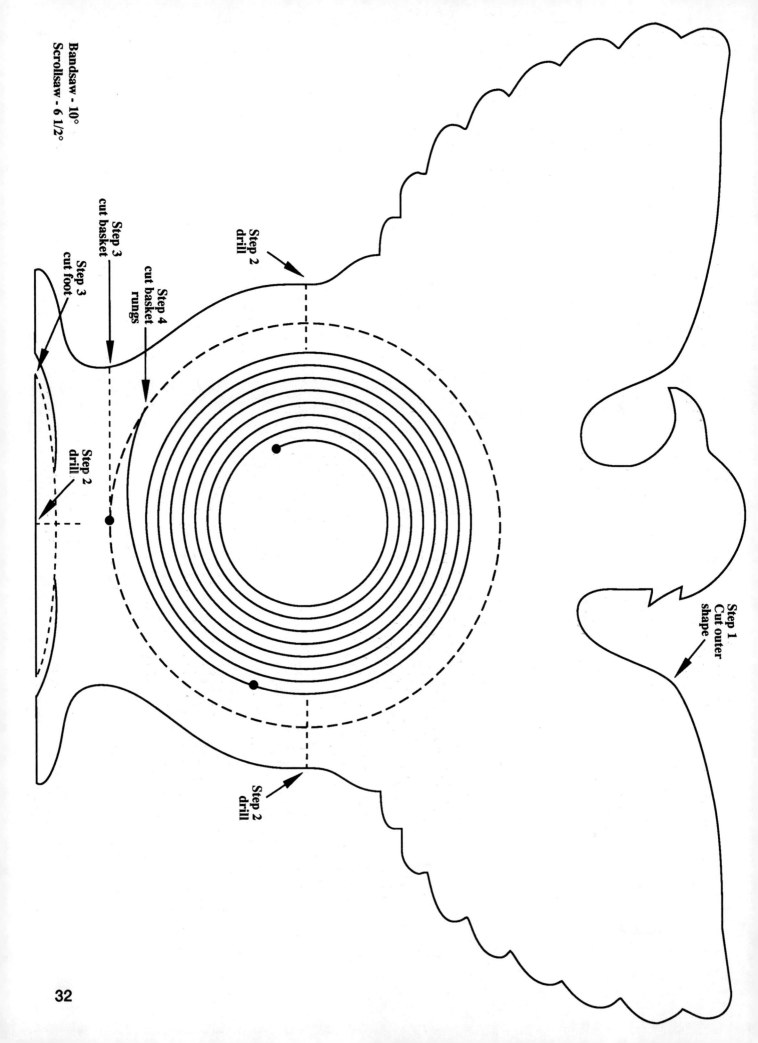

Bandsaw - 10°
Scrollsaw - 6 1/2°

Step 3
cut basket

Step 3
cut foot

Step 2
drill

Step 4
cut basket
rungs

Step 2
drill

Step 2
drill

Step 2
drill

Step 1
Cut outer
shape

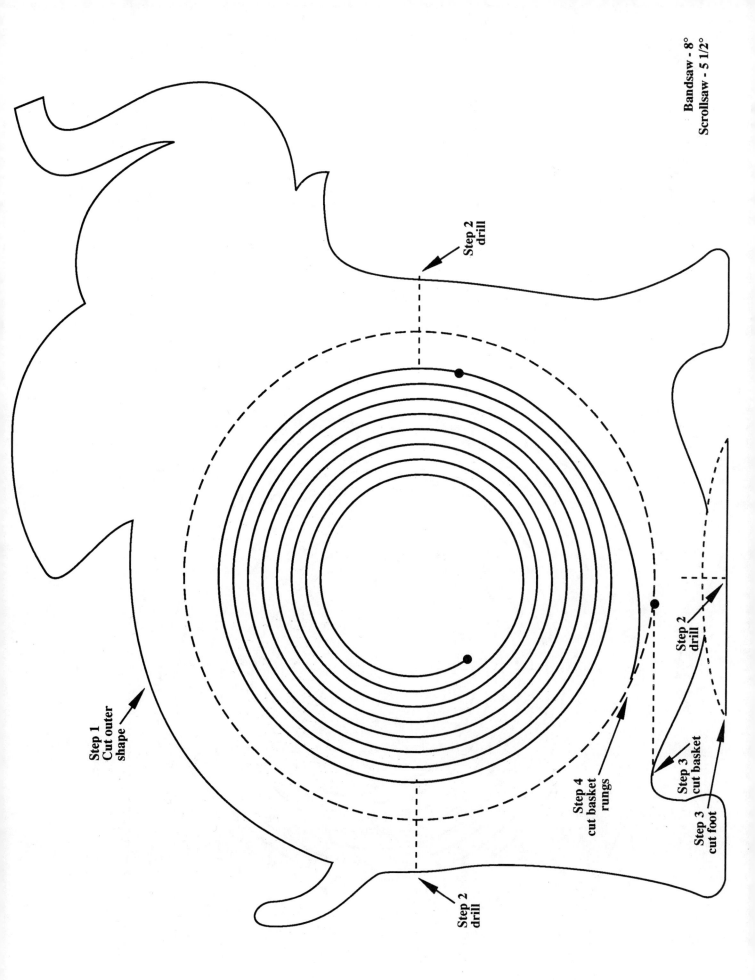

Bandsaw - 8°
Scrollsaw - 5 1/2°

Step 2
drill

Step 1
Cut outer
shape

Step 4
cut basket
rungs

Step 2
drill

Step 3
cut basket

Step 3
cut foot

Step 2
drill

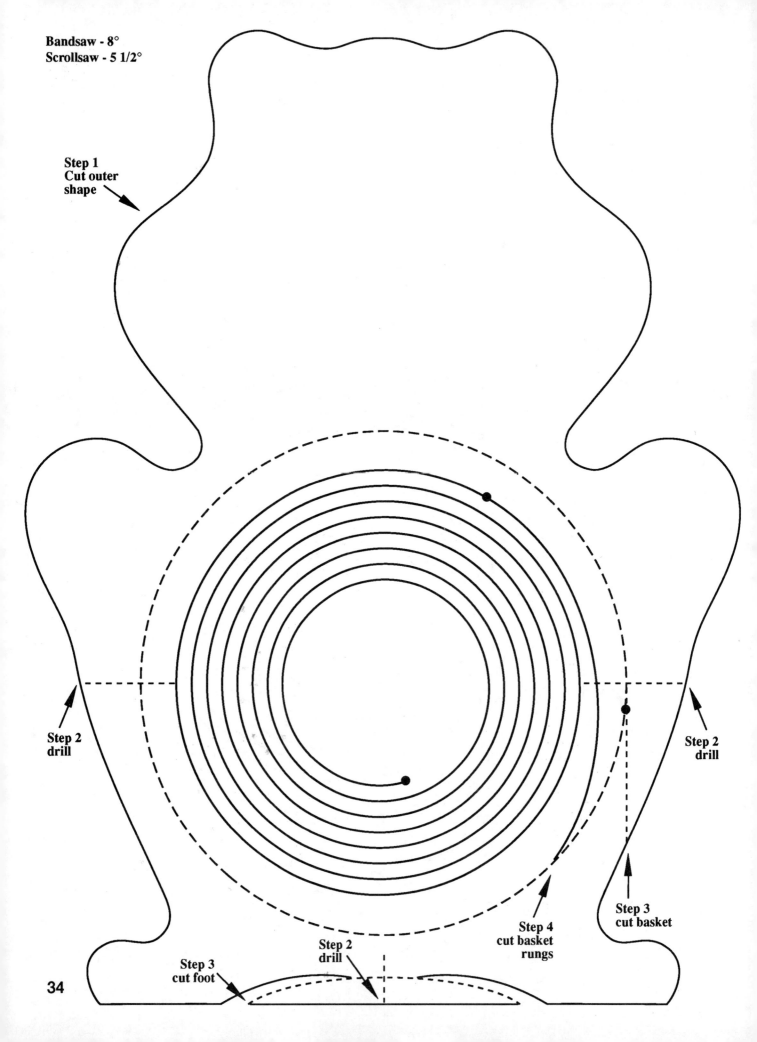

Bandsaw - 8°
Scrollsaw - 5 1/2°

Step 1
Cut outer
shape

Step 2
drill

Step 2
drill

Step 2
drill

Step 3
cut foot

Step 3
cut basket

Step 4
cut basket
rungs

34

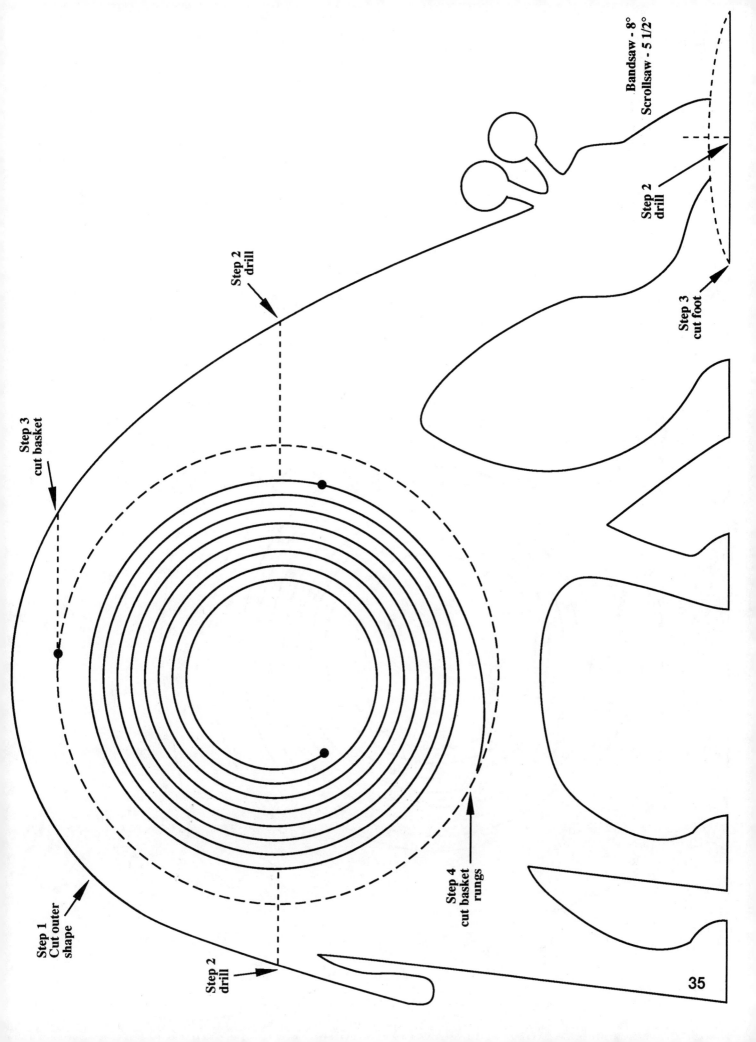

Bandsaw - 8°
Scrollsaw - 5 1/2°

Step 2
drill

Step 3
cut foot

Step 2
drill

Step 3
cut basket

Step 1
Cut outer
shape

Step 4
cut basket
rungs

Step 2
drill

35

Step 1
Cut outer
shape

Step 2
drill

Step 3
cut basket

Step 4
cut basket
rungs

Step 3
cut foot

Step 2
drill

Step 2
drill

Bandsaw - 8°
Scrollsaw - 5 1/2°

36

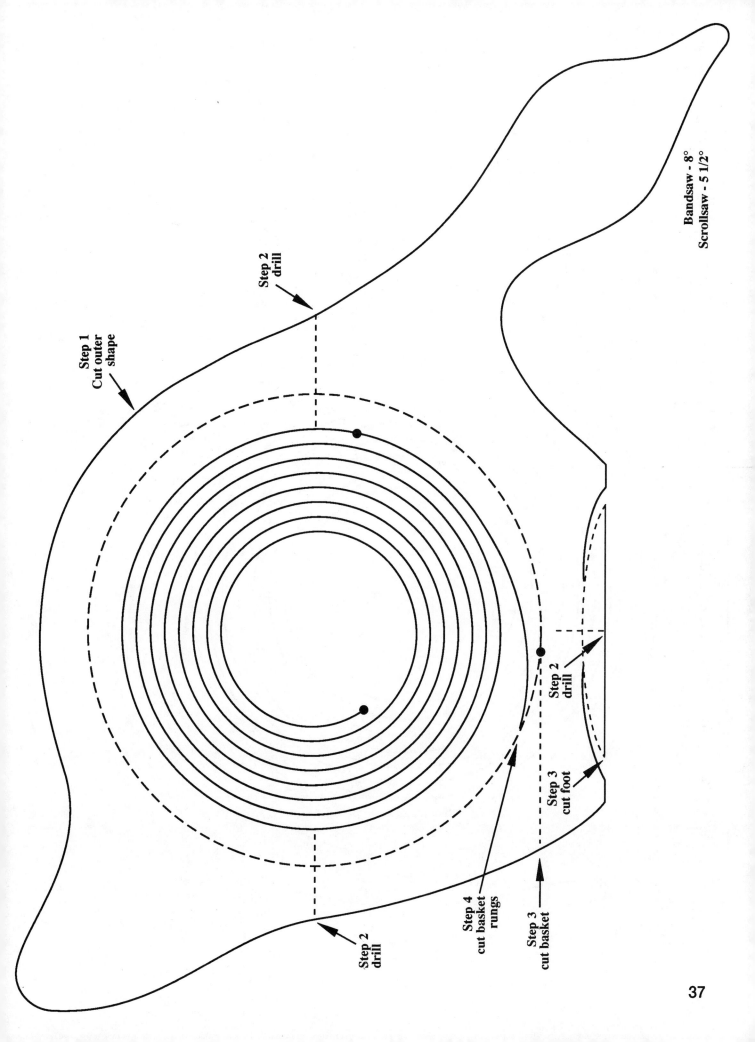

Step 1
Cut outer
shape

Step 2
drill

Step 2
drill

Bandsaw - 8°
Scrollsaw - 5 1/2°

Step 2
drill

Step 3
cut foot

Step 4
cut basket
rungs

Step 3
cut basket

37

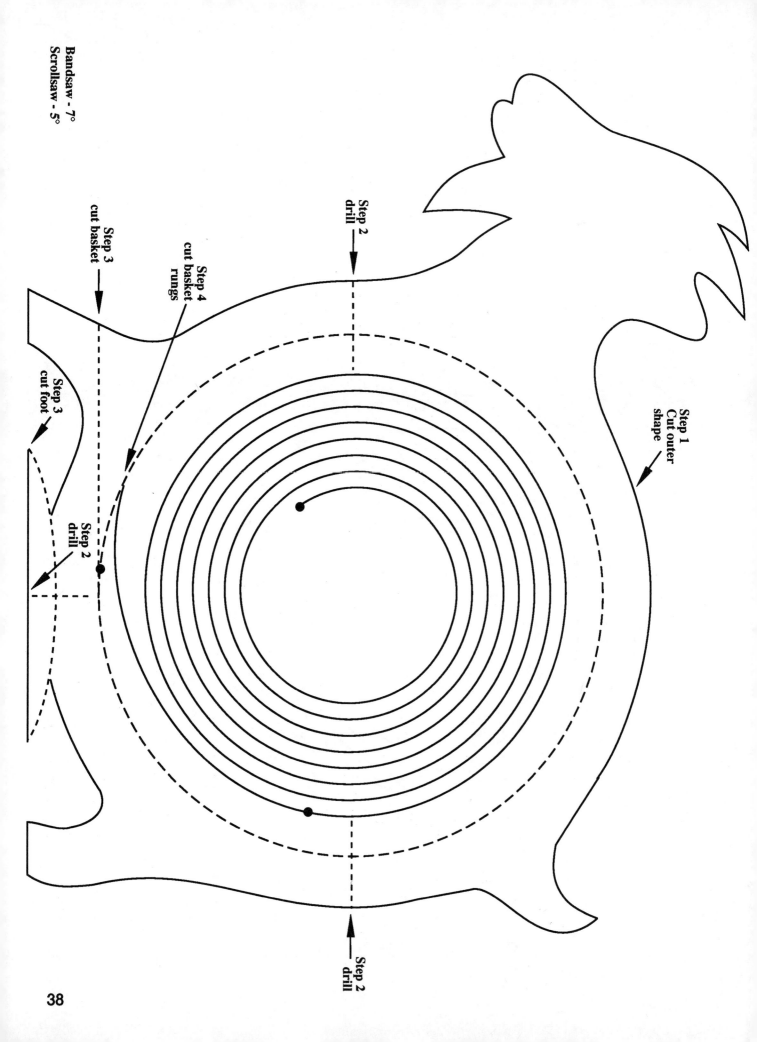

Bandsaw - 7°
Scrollsaw - 5°

Step 1
Cut outer
shape

Step 2
drill

Step 2
drill

Step 2
drill

Step 3
cut basket

Step 4
cut basket
rungs

Step 3
cut foot

38

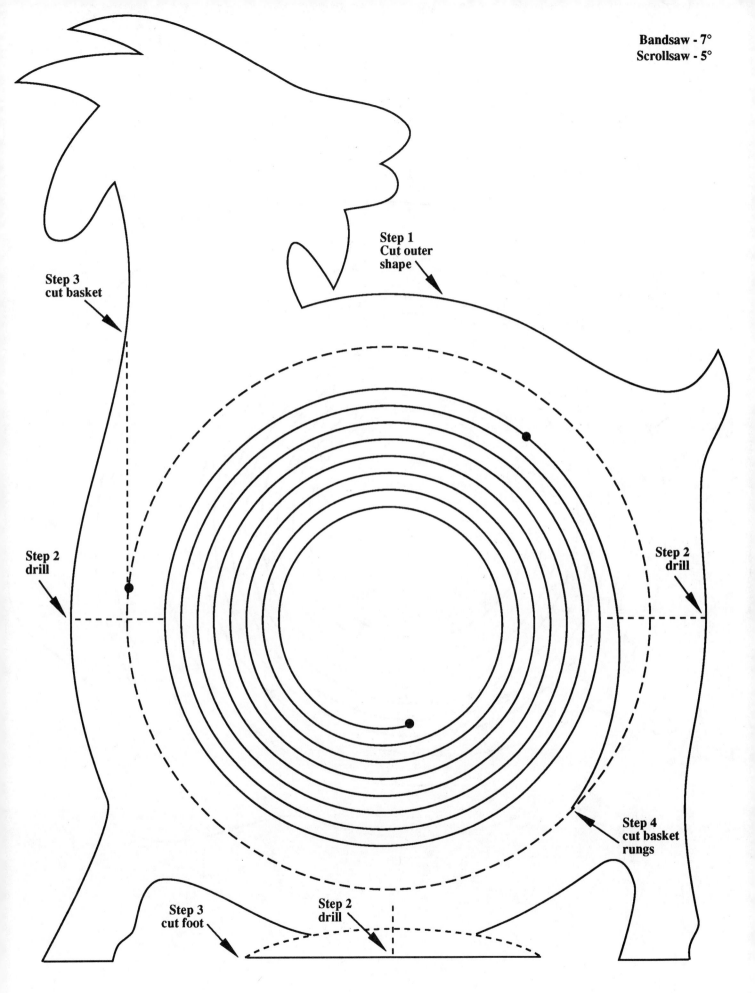

Bandsaw - 7°
Scrollsaw - 5°

Step 1
Cut outer
shape

Step 3
cut basket

Step 2
drill

Step 2
drill

Step 4
cut basket
rungs

Step 3
cut foot

Step 2
drill

39

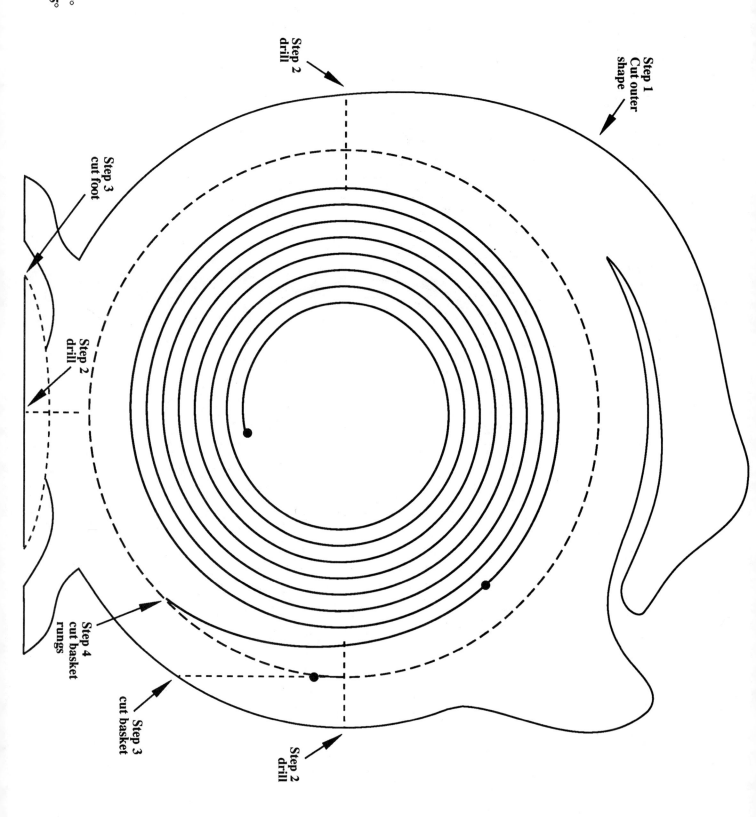

Bandsaw - 7°
Scrollsaw - 5°

Step 1
Cut outer
shape

Step 2
drill

Step 3
cut foot

Step 2
drill

Step 4
cut basket
rungs

Step 3
cut basket

Step 2
drill

40

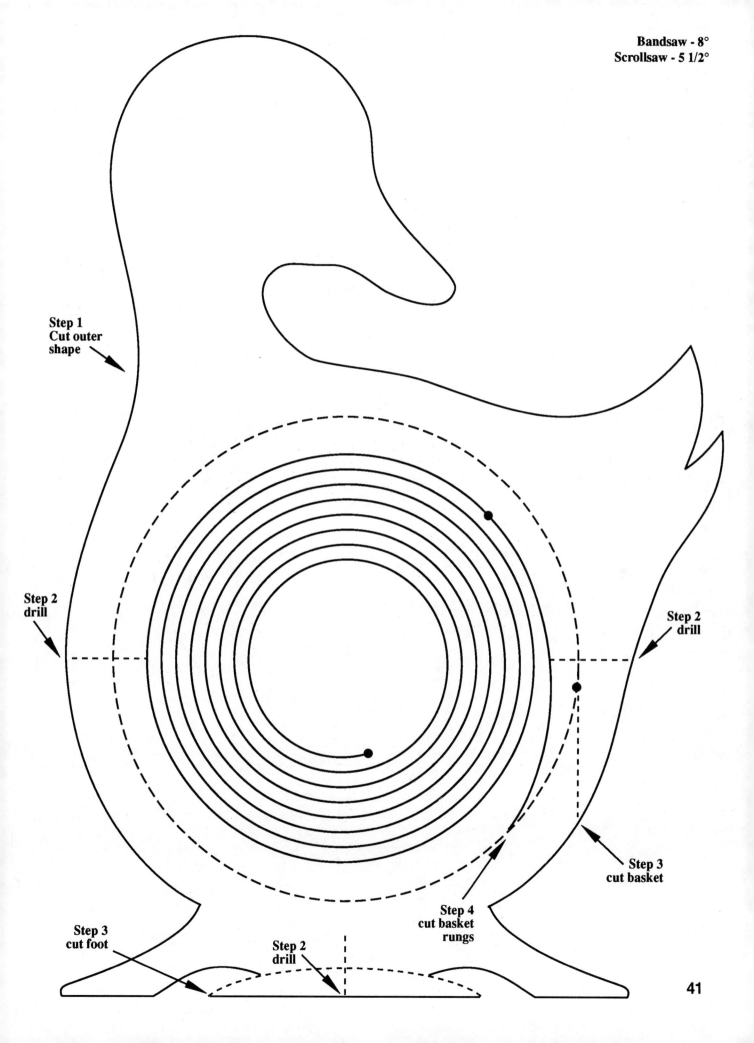

Bandsaw - 8°
Scrollsaw - 5 1/2°

Step 1
Cut outer
shape

Step 2
drill

Step 2
drill

Step 3
cut basket

Step 4
cut basket
rungs

Step 3
cut foot

Step 2
drill

41

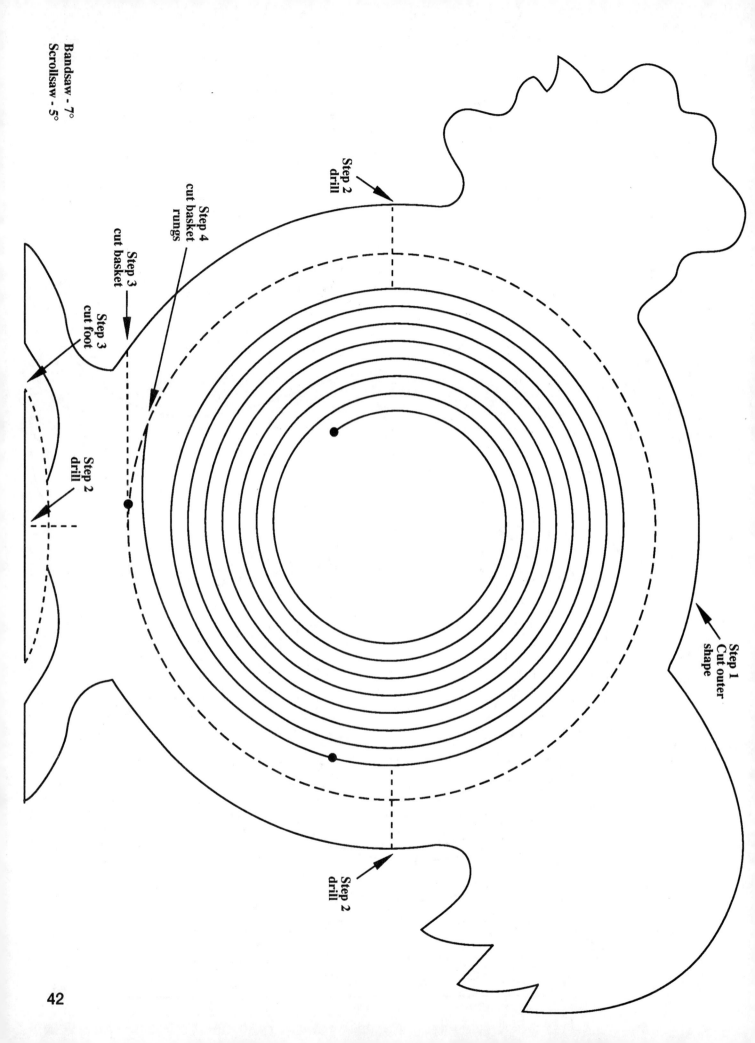

Bandsaw - 7°
Scrollsaw - 5°

Step 2
drill

Step 4
cut basket
rungs

Step 3
cut basket

Step 3
cut foot

Step 2
drill

Step 1
Cut outer
shape

Step 2
drill

42

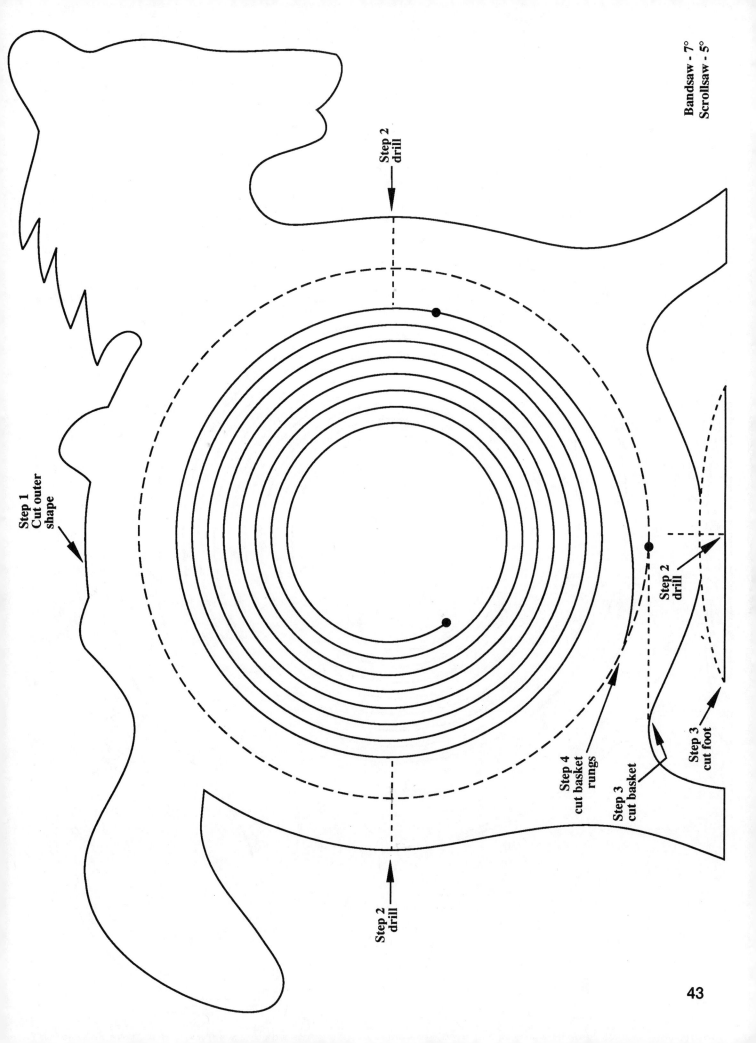

Step 1
Cut outer
shape

Step 2
drill

Step 2
drill

Step 2
drill

Step 4
cut basket
rungs

Step 3
cut basket

Step 3
cut foot

Bandsaw - 7°
Scrollsaw - 5°

43

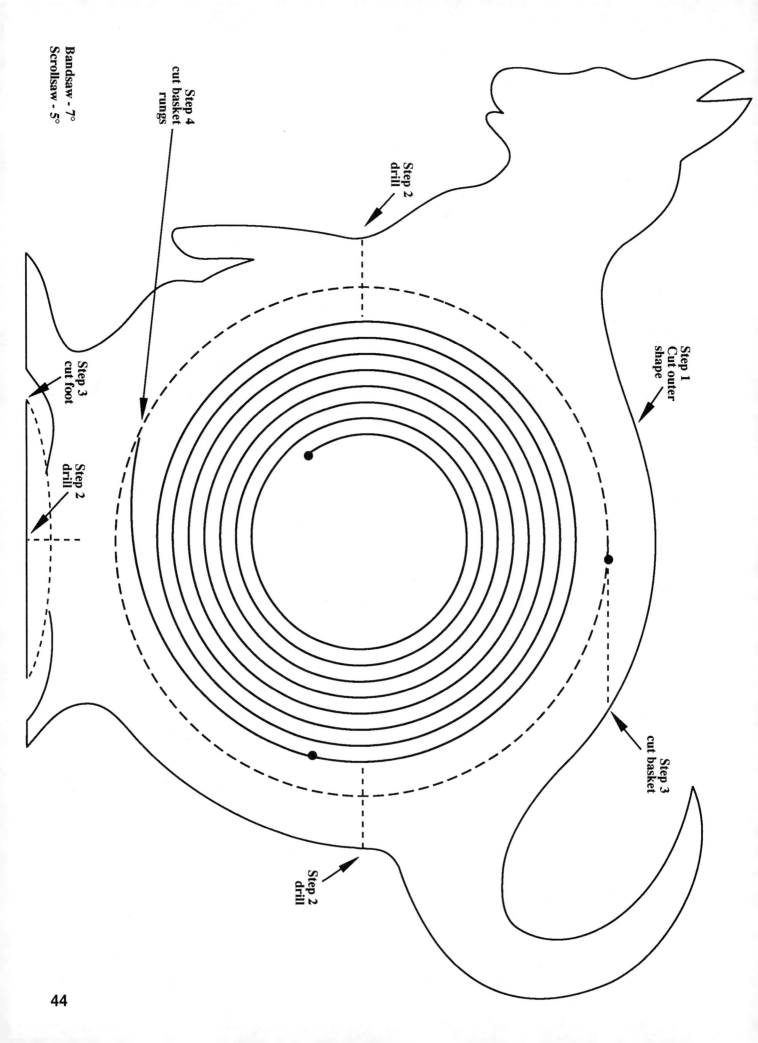

Step 2
drill

Step 1
Cut outer
shape

Step 3
cut basket

Step 2
drill

Step 3
cut foot

Step 2
drill

Step 4
cut basket
rungs

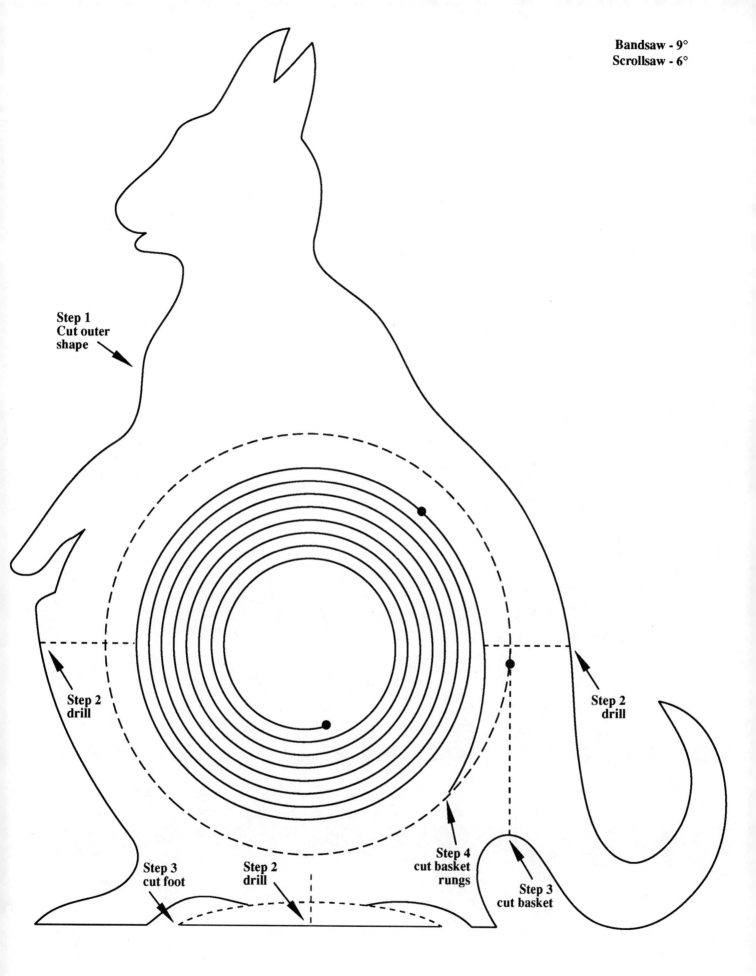

Bandsaw - 9°
Scrollsaw - 6°

Step 1
Cut outer
shape

Step 2
drill

Step 2
drill

Step 3
cut foot

Step 2
drill

Step 4
cut basket
rungs

Step 3
cut basket

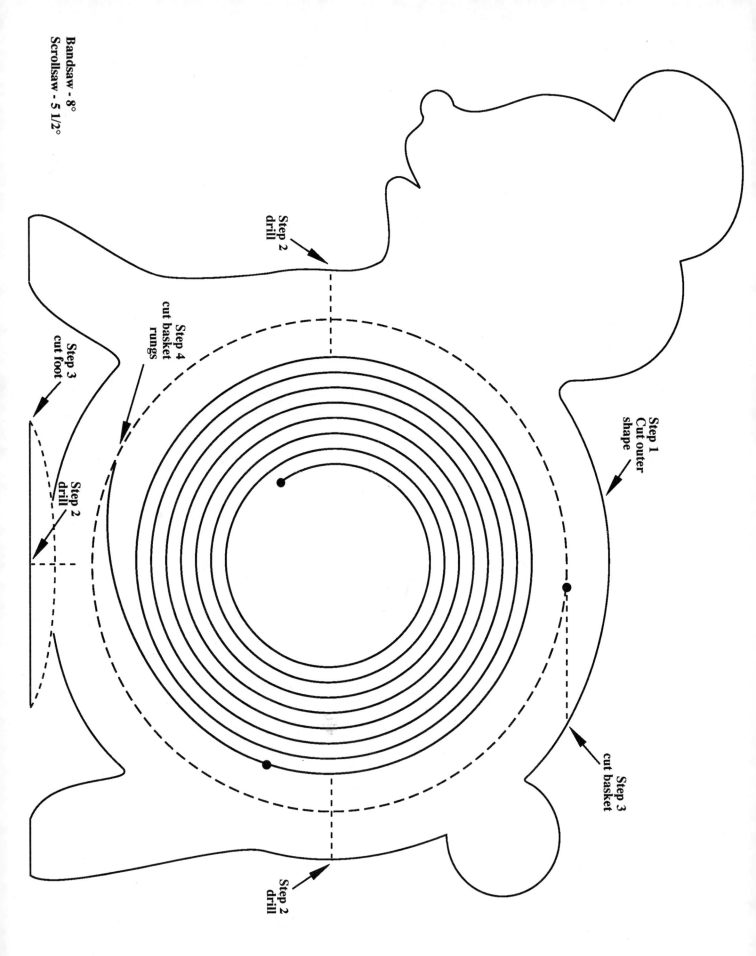

Bandsaw - 8°
Scrollsaw - 5 1/2°

Step 2
drill

Step 4
cut basket
rungs

Step 3
cut foot

Step 2
drill

Step 1
Cut outer
shape

Step 3
cut basket

Step 2
drill

46

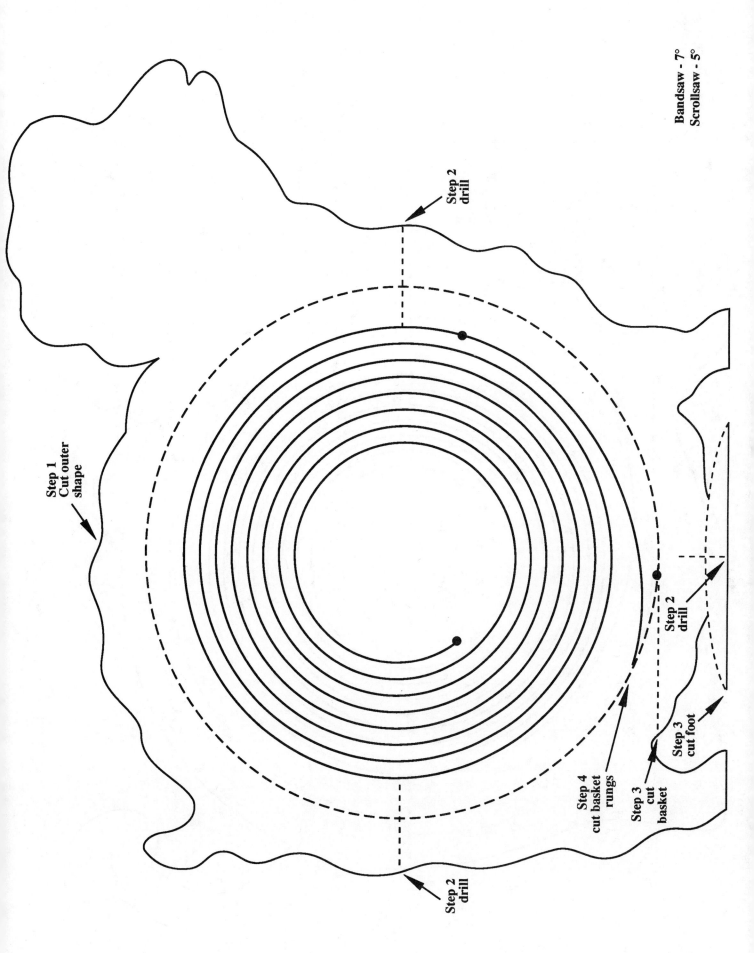

Bandsaw - 7°
Scrollsaw - 5°

Step 2
drill

Step 1
Cut outer
shape

Step 2
drill

Step 4
cut basket
rungs

Step 3
cut
basket

Step 2
drill

Step 3
cut foot

Bandsaw - 8°
Scrollsaw - 5 1/2°

Step 3
cut basket

Step 4
cut basket
rungs

Step 2
drill

Step 3
cut foot

Step 2
drill

Step 1
Cut outer
shape

Step 2
drill

48

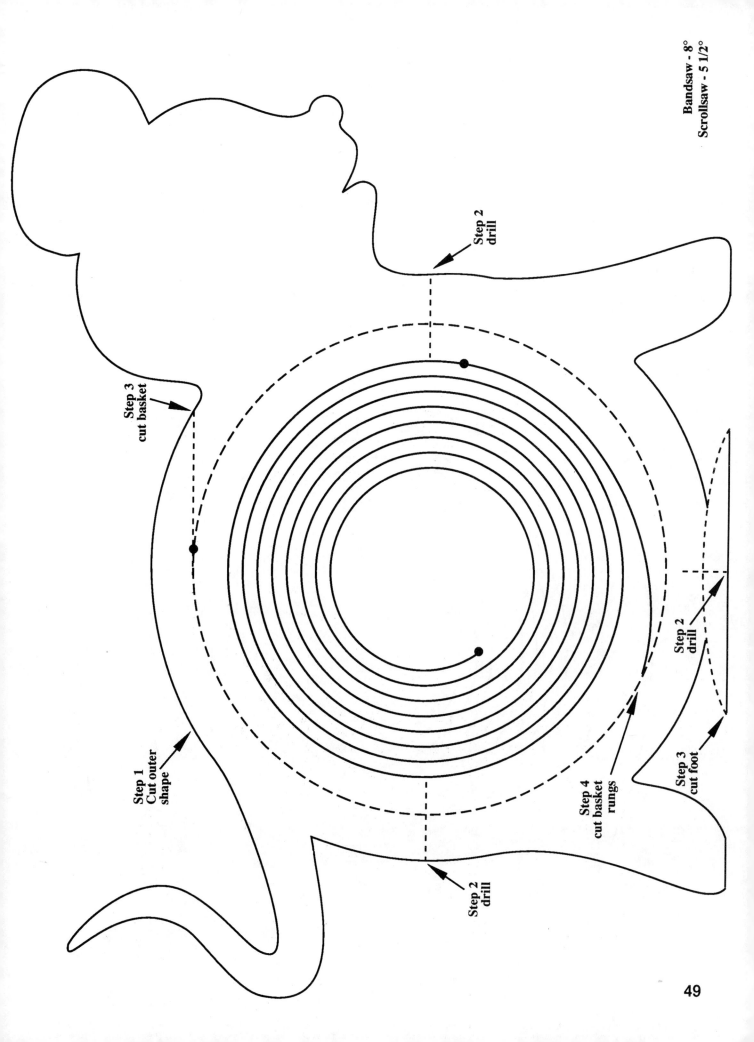

Bandsaw - 8°
Scrollsaw - 5 1/2°

Step 2
drill

Step 3
cut basket

Step 1
Cut outer
shape

Step 4
cut basket
rungs

Step 2
drill

Step 3
cut foot

Step 2
drill

49

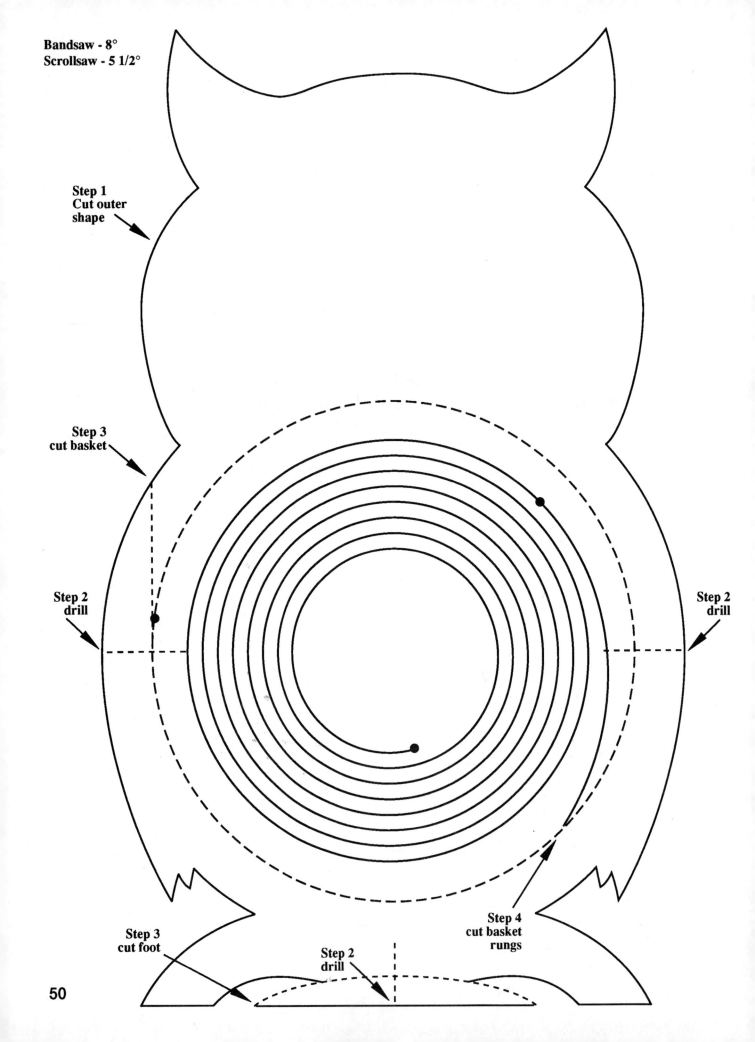

Bandsaw - 8°
Scrollsaw - 5 1/2°

Step 1
Cut outer
shape

Step 3
cut basket

Step 2
drill

Step 2
drill

Step 4
cut basket
rungs

Step 3
cut foot

Step 2
drill

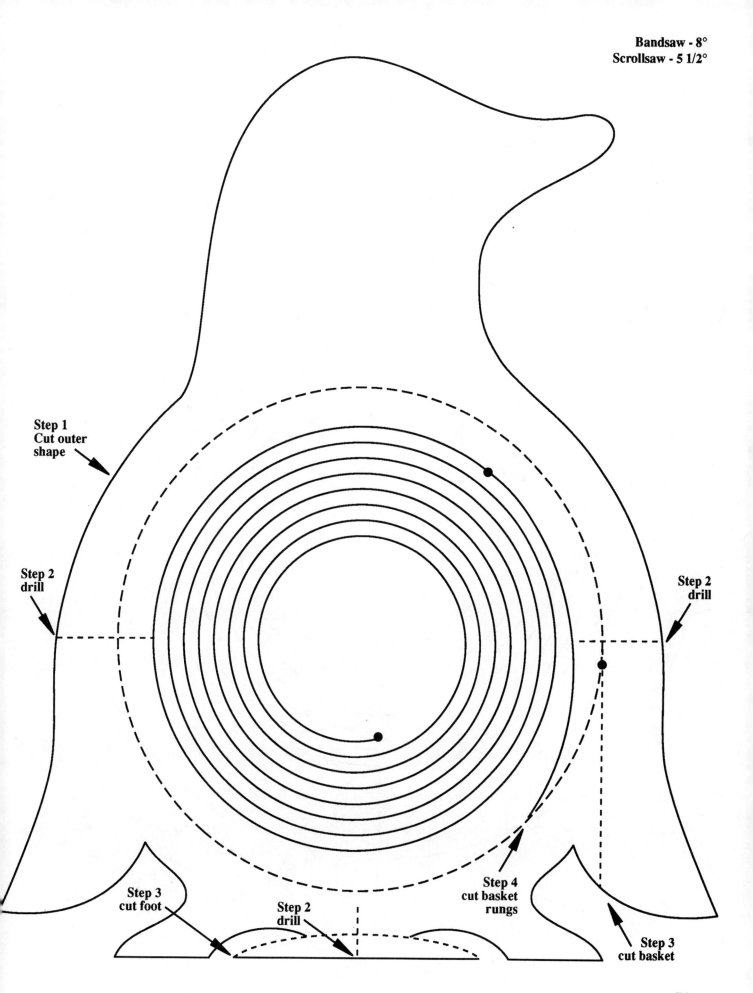

Bandsaw - 8°
Scrollsaw - 5 1/2°

Step 1
Cut outer
shape

Step 2
drill

Step 2
drill

Step 4
cut basket
rungs

Step 3
cut foot

Step 2
drill

Step 3
cut basket

51

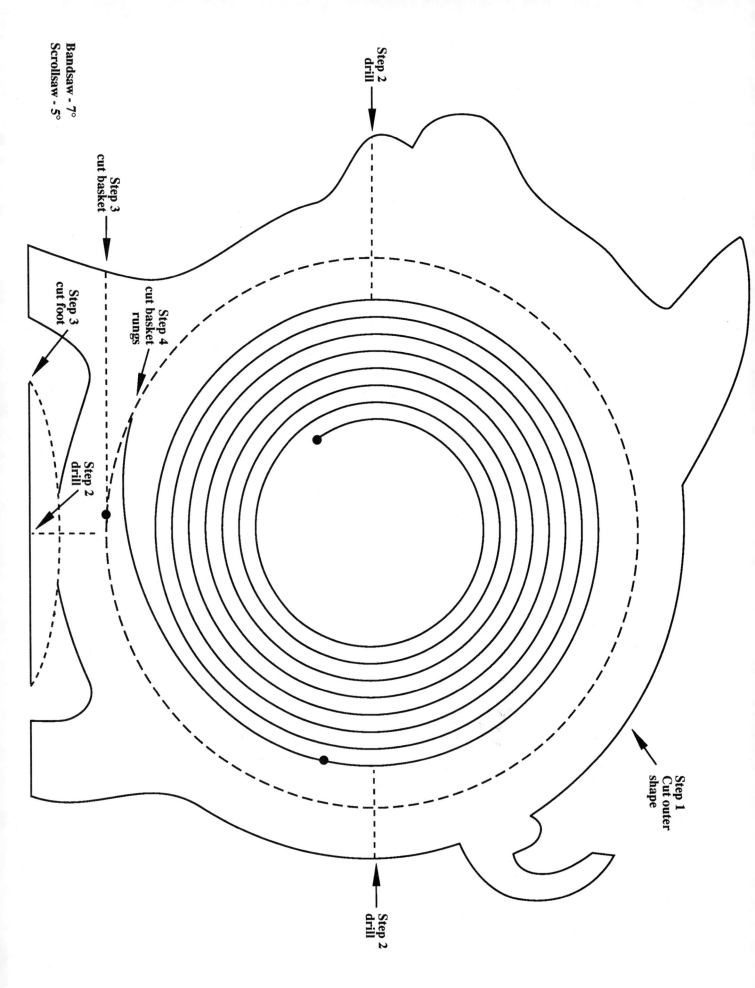

Step 2
drill

Step 3
cut basket

Step 3
cut foot

Step 4
cut basket
rungs

Step 2
drill

Step 2
drill

Step 1
Cut outer
shape

Step 2
drill

Bandsaw - 7°
Scrollsaw - 5°

52

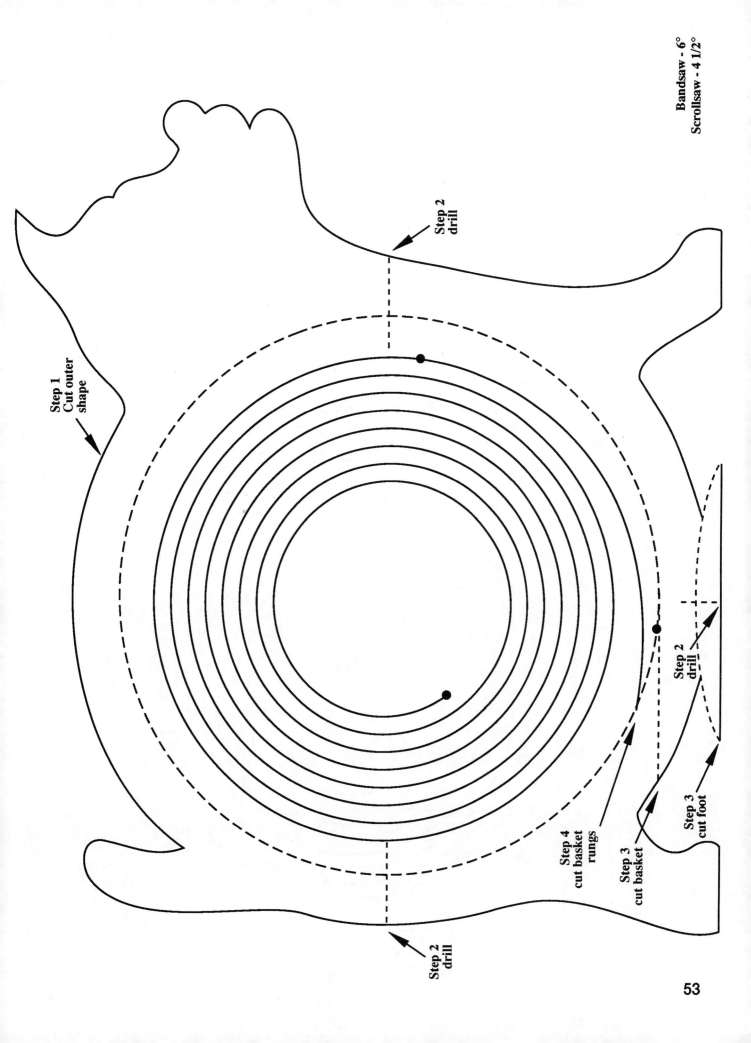

Step 2
drill

Step 1
Cut outer
shape

Step 2
drill

Step 4
cut basket
rungs

Step 3
cut basket

Step 3
cut foot

Step 2
drill

Bandsaw - 6°
Scrollsaw - 4 1/2°

53

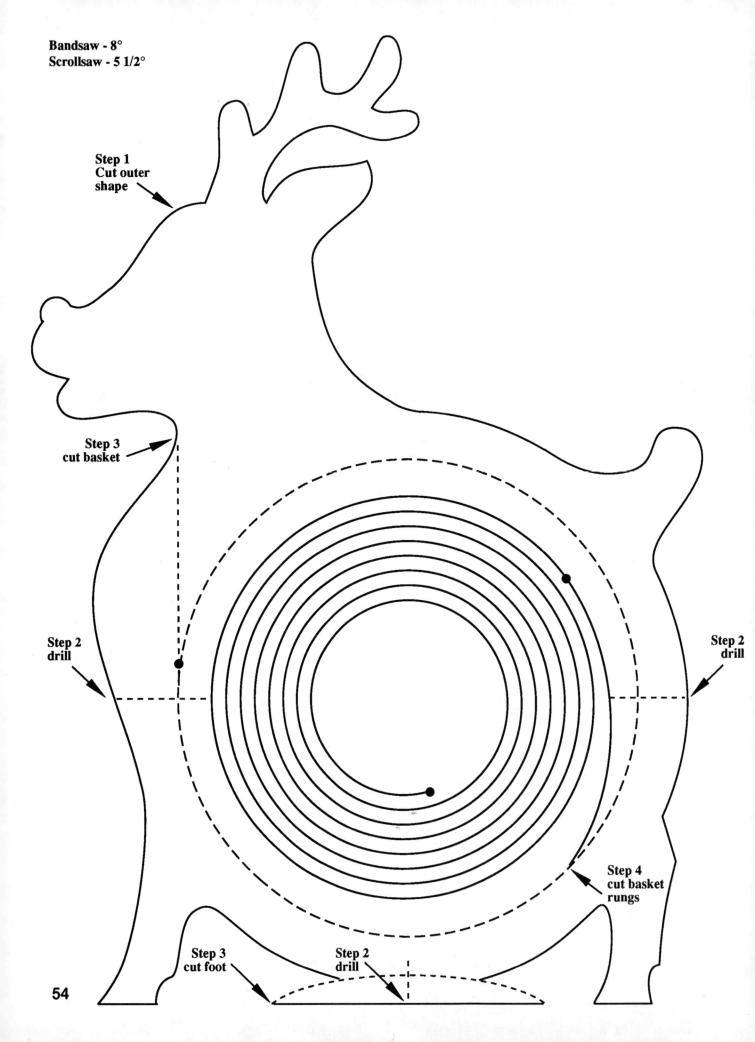

Bandsaw - 8°
Scrollsaw - 5 1/2°

Step 1
Cut outer
shape

Step 3
cut basket

Step 2
drill

Step 2
drill

Step 4
cut basket
rungs

Step 3
cut foot

Step 2
drill

54

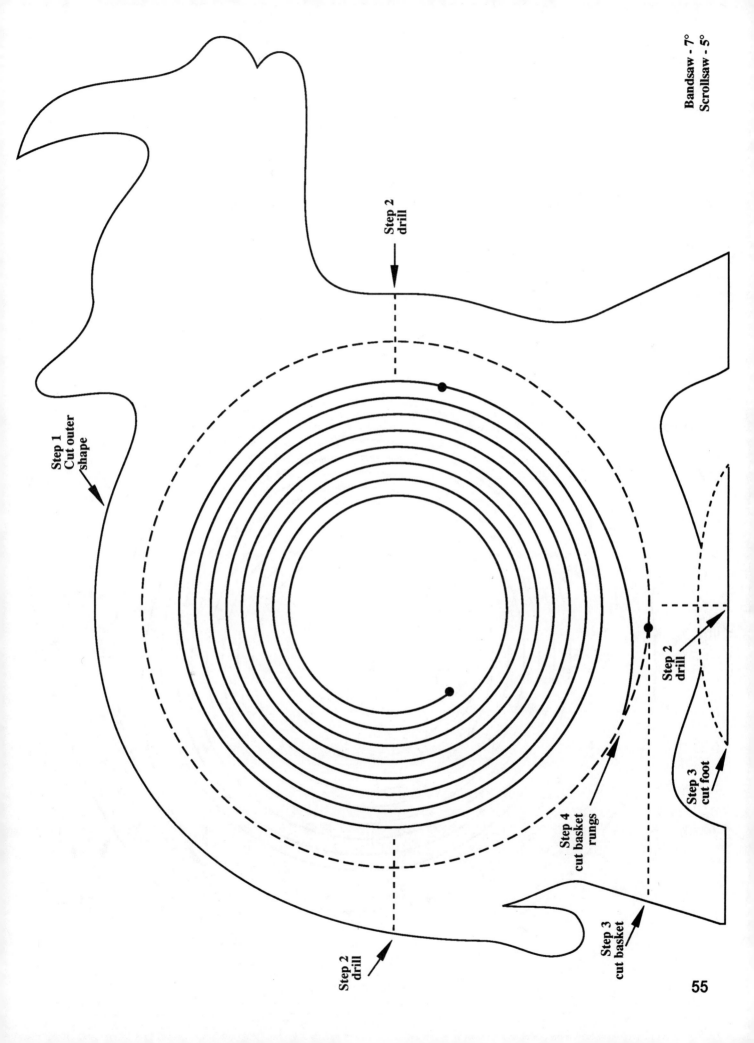

Bandsaw - 7°
Scrollsaw - 5°

Step 2
drill

Step 1
Cut outer
shape

Step 2
drill

Step 2
drill

Step 4
cut basket
rungs

Step 3
cut foot

Step 3
cut basket

55

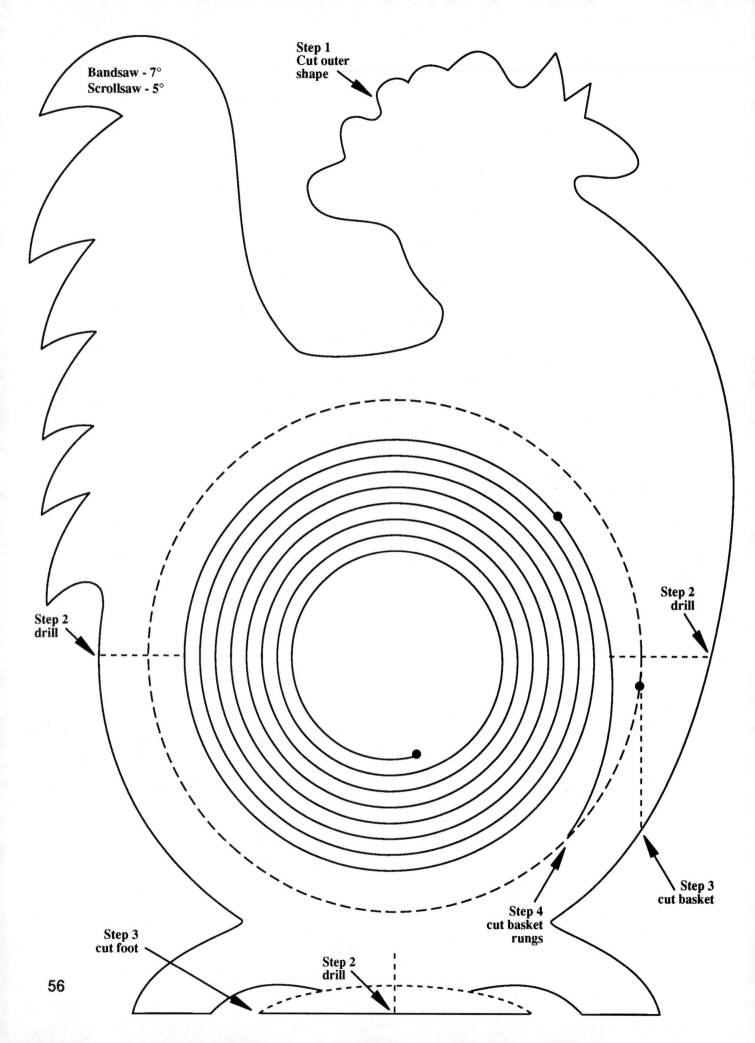

Bandsaw - 7°
Scrollsaw - 5°

Step 1
Cut outer
shape

Step 2
drill

Step 2
drill

Step 3
cut basket

Step 4
cut basket
rungs

Step 3
cut foot

Step 2
drill

56

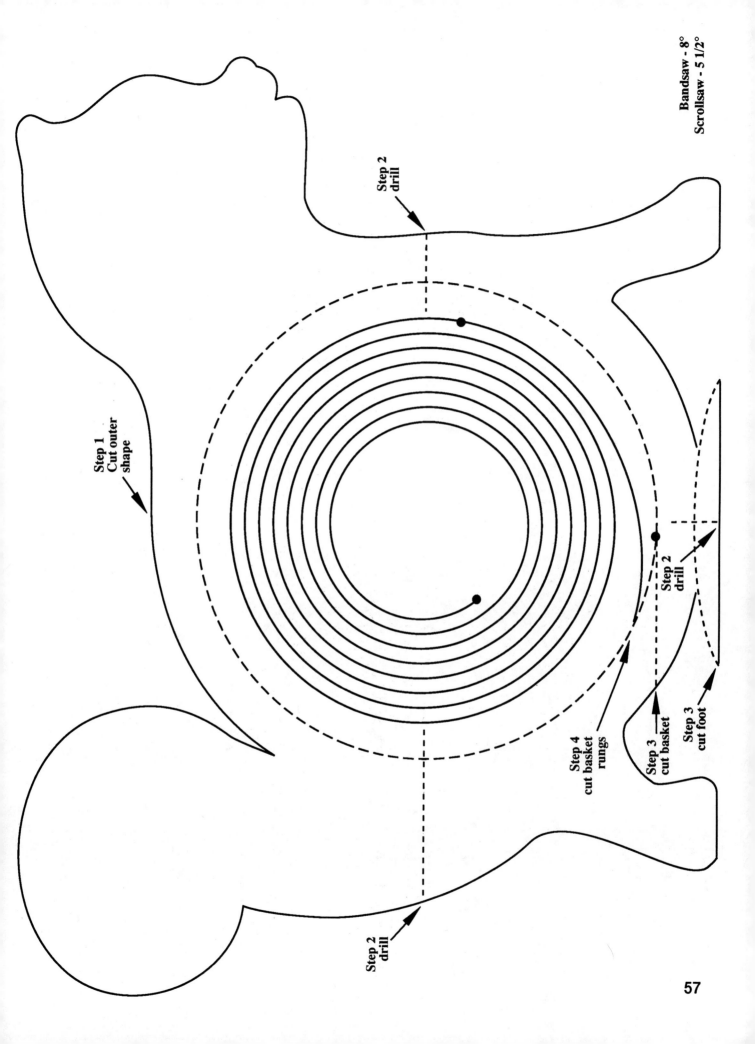

Step 2
drill

Step 1
Cut outer
shape

Step 4
cut basket
rungs

Step 3
cut basket

Step 2
drill

Step 3
cut foot

Step 2
drill

Bandsaw - 8°
Scrollsaw - 5 1/2°

57

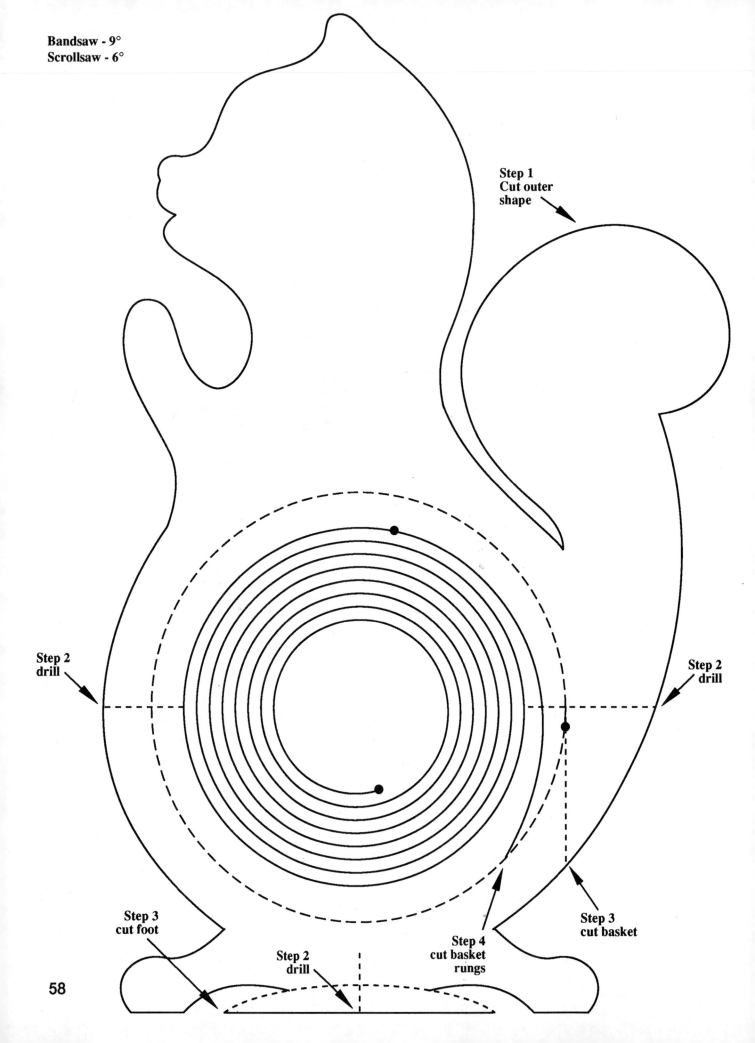

Bandsaw - 9°
Scrollsaw - 6°

Step 1
Cut outer
shape

Step 2
drill

Step 2
drill

Step 3
cut foot

Step 2
drill

Step 4
cut basket
rungs

Step 3
cut basket

58

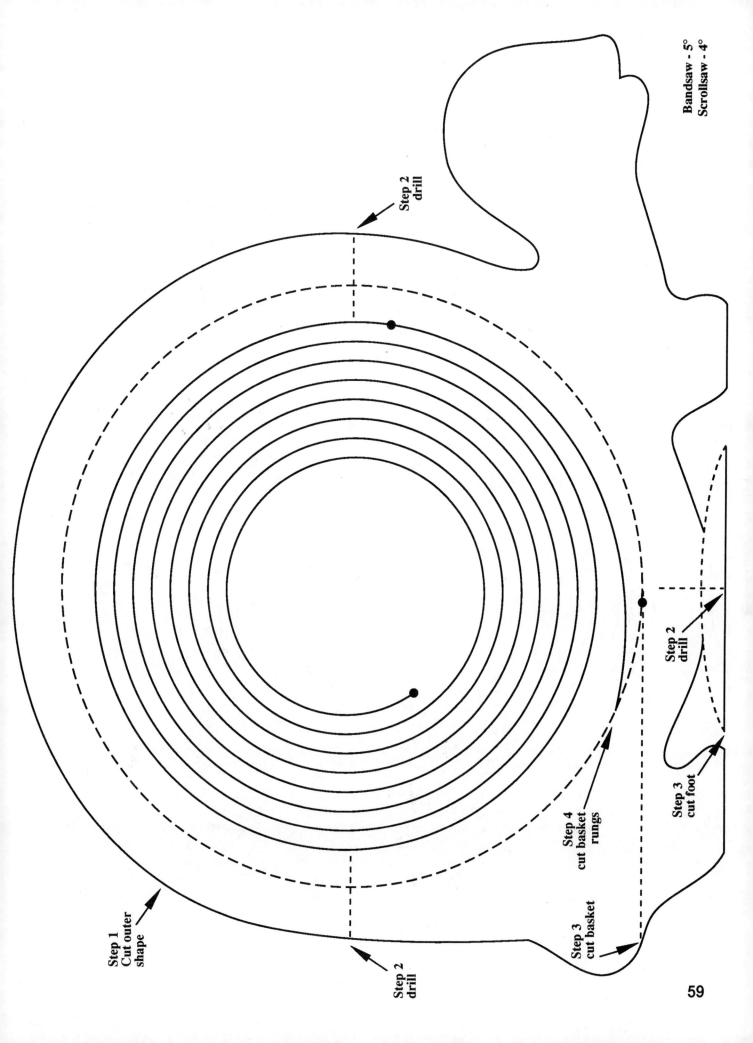

Step 2
drill

Bandsaw - 5°
Scrollsaw - 4°

Step 2
drill

Step 2
drill

Step 1
Cut outer
shape

Step 4
cut basket
rungs

Step 3
cut basket

Step 3
cut foot

59

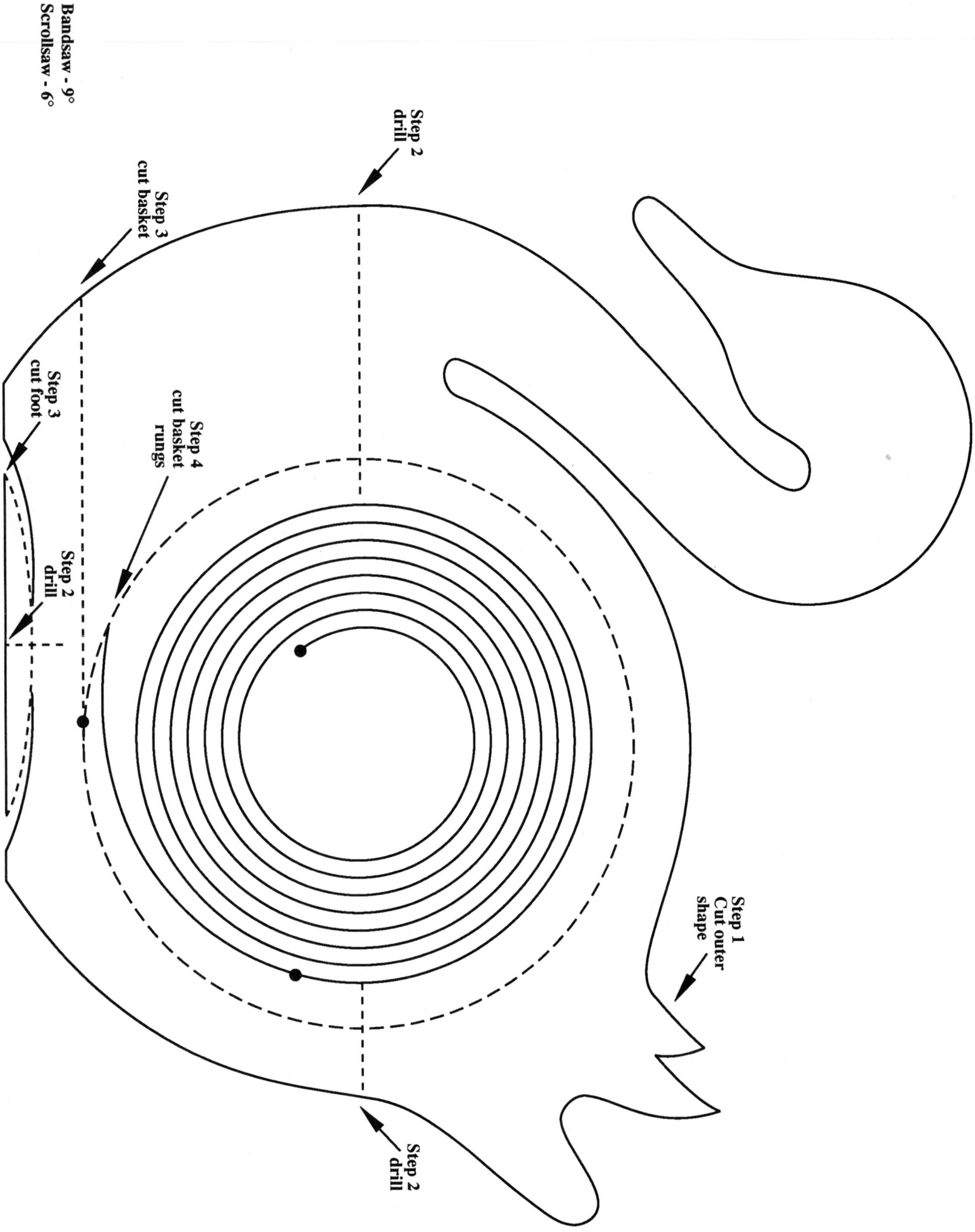

Step 2
drill

Step 3
cut basket

Step 3
cut foot

Step 4
cut basket
rungs

Step 2
drill

Step 1
Cut outer
shape

Step 2
drill

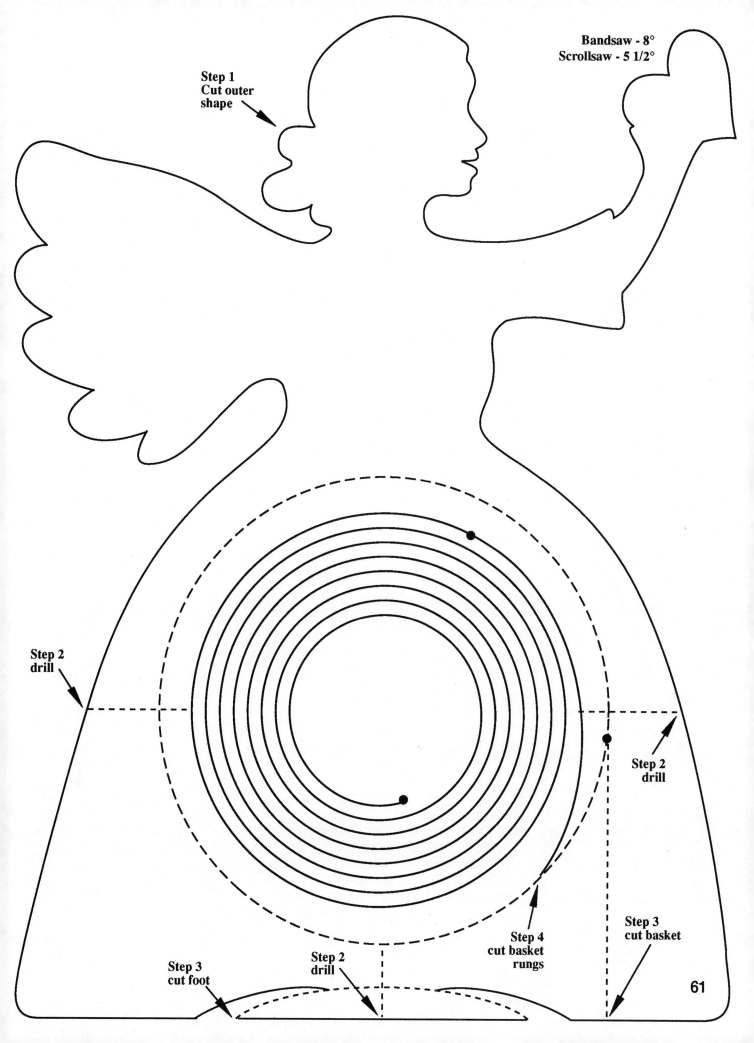

Bandsaw - 8°
Scrollsaw - 5 1/2°

Step 1
Cut outer
shape

Step 2
drill

Step 2
drill

Step 4
cut basket
rungs

Step 3
cut basket

Step 3
cut foot

Step 2
drill

61

Bandsaw - 8°
Scrollsaw - 5 1/2°

Step 1
Cut outer
shape

Step 2
drill

Step 2
drill

Step 4
cut basket
rungs

Step 3
cut basket

Step 3
cut foot

Step 2
drill

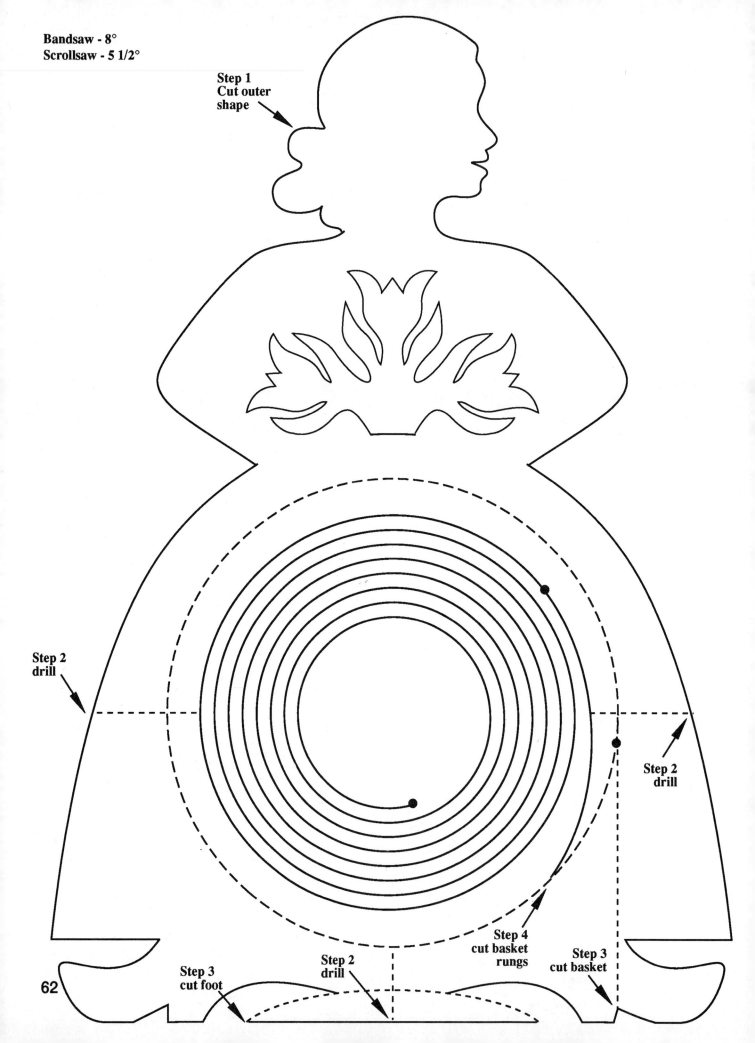

62

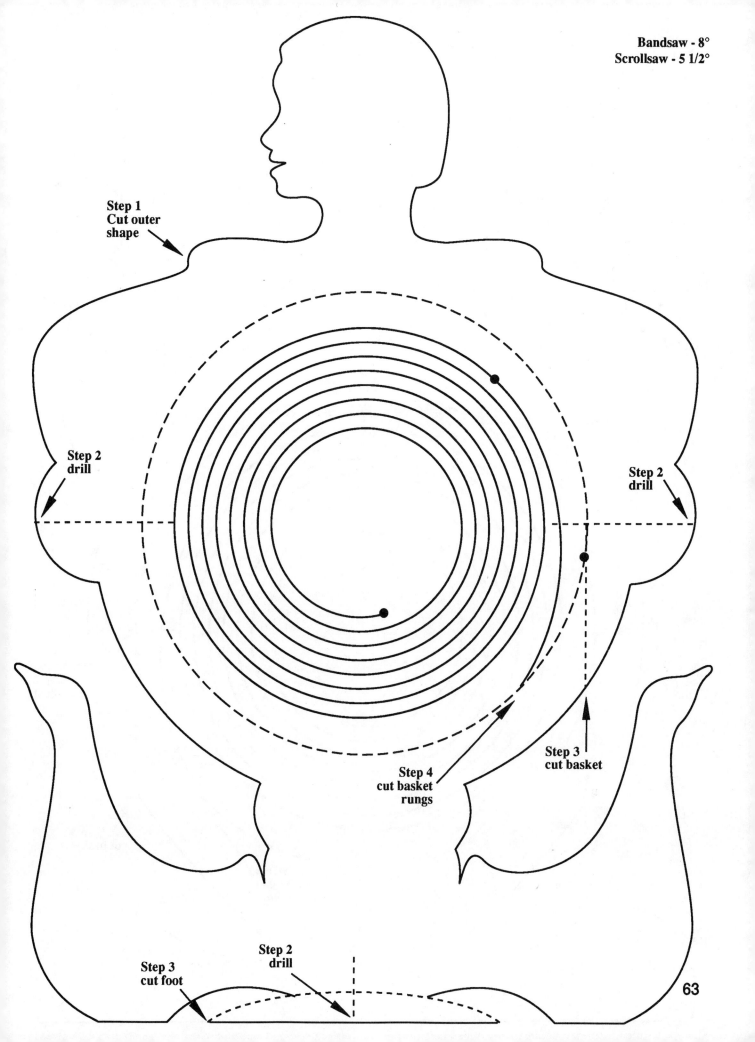

Bandsaw - 8°
Scrollsaw - 5 1/2°

Step 1
Cut outer
shape

Step 2
drill

Step 2
drill

Step 3
cut basket

Step 4
cut basket
rungs

Step 3
cut foot

Step 2
drill

63

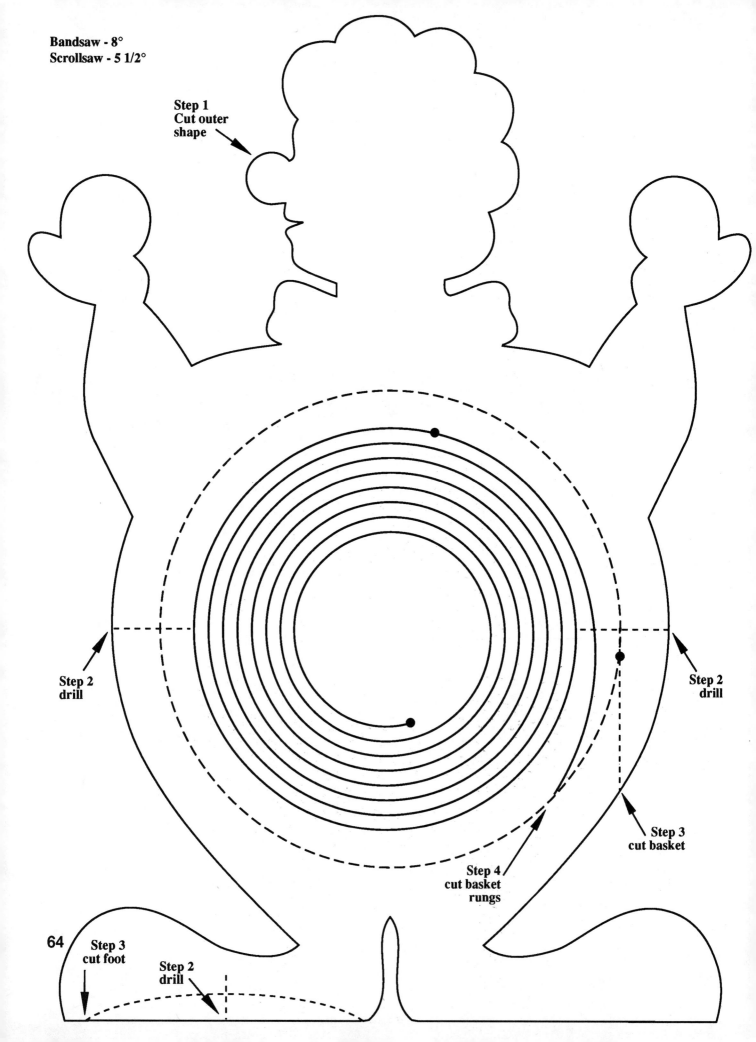

Bandsaw - 8°
Scrollsaw - 5 1/2°

Step 1
Cut outer
shape

Step 2
drill

Step 2
drill

Step 3
cut basket

Step 4
cut basket
rungs

64

Step 3
cut foot

Step 2
drill

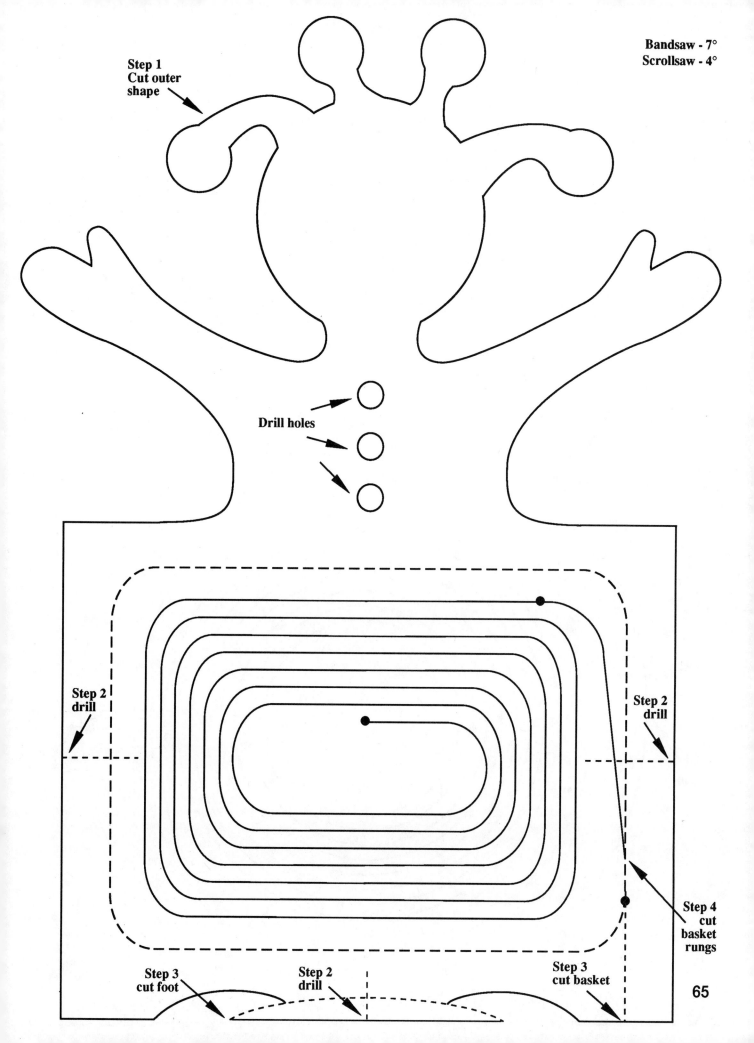

Bandsaw - 7°
Scrollsaw - 4°

Step 1
Cut outer
shape

Drill holes

Step 2
drill

Step 2
drill

Step 4
cut
basket
rungs

Step 3
cut foot

Step 2
drill

Step 3
cut basket

65

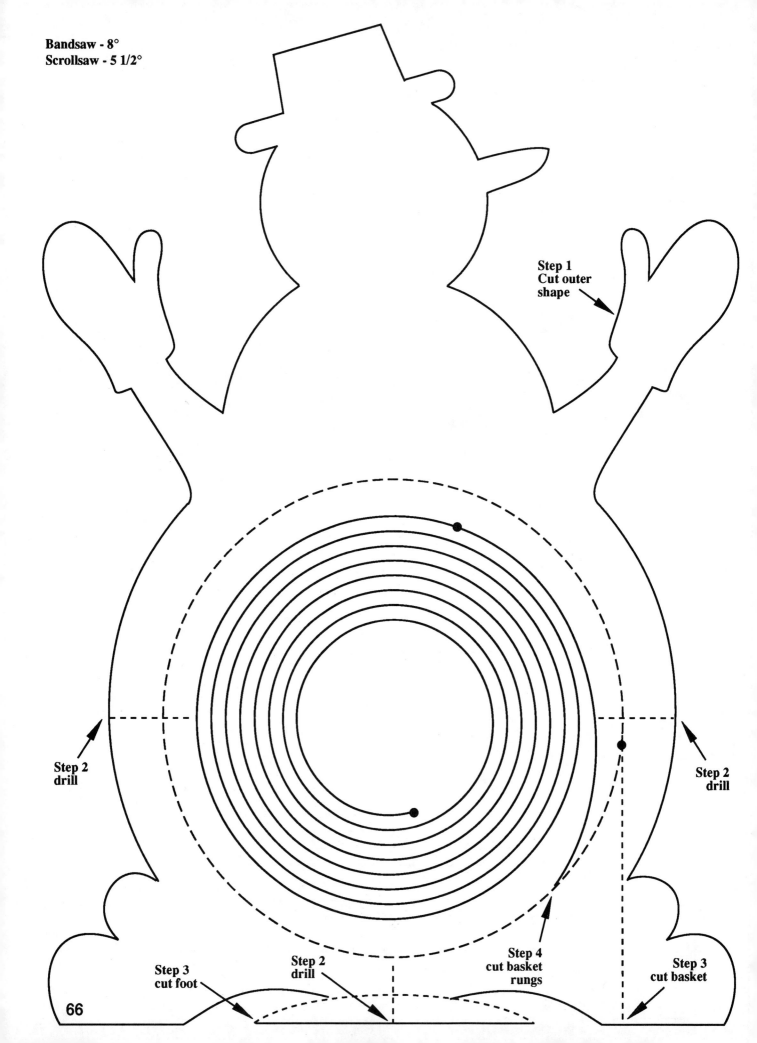

Bandsaw - 8°
Scrollsaw - 5 1/2°

Step 1
Cut outer
shape

Step 2
drill

Step 2
drill

Step 4
cut basket
rungs

Step 3
cut foot

Step 2
drill

Step 3
cut basket

66

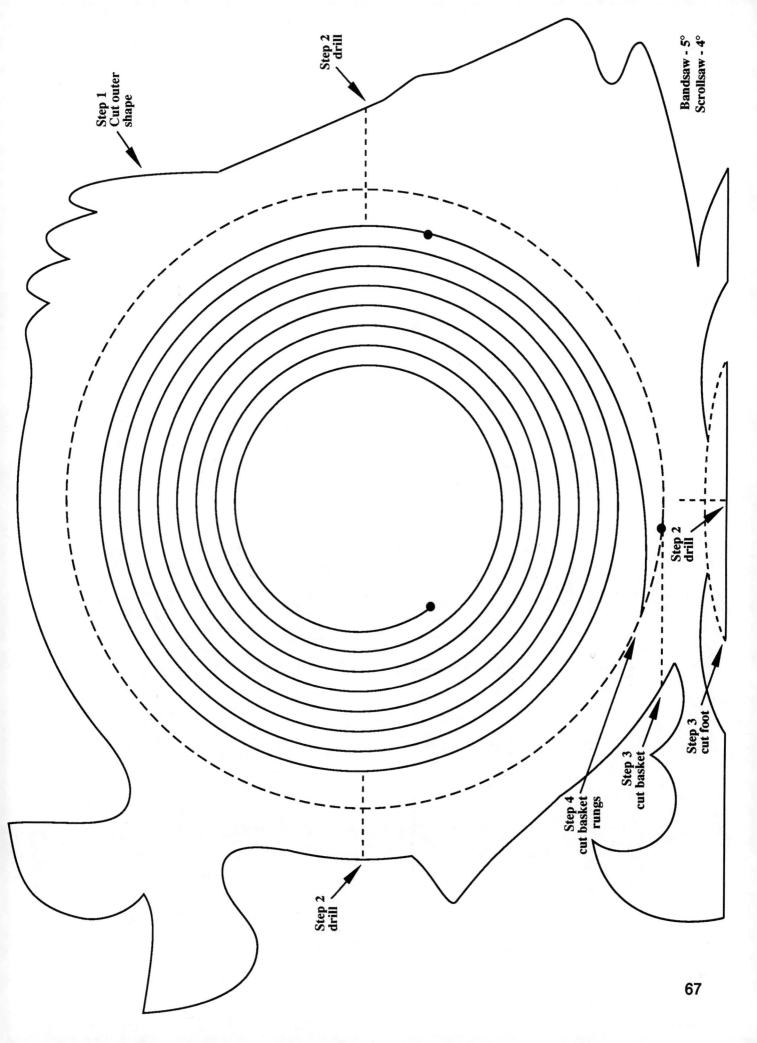

Step 1
Cut outer
shape

Step 2 drill

Bandsaw - 5°
Scrollsaw - 4°

Step 2
drill

Step 2
drill

Step 4
cut basket
rungs

Step 3
cut basket

Step 3
cut foot

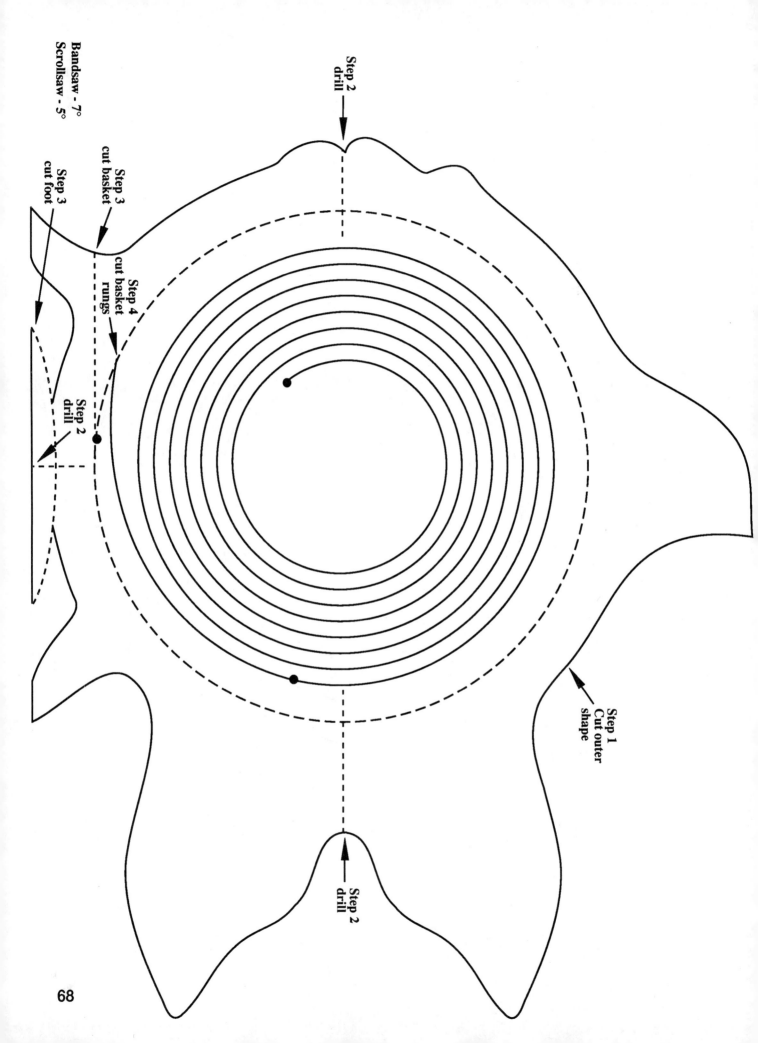

Step 2
drill

Step 3
cut basket

Step 3
cut foot

Step 4
cut basket
rungs

Step 2
drill

Step 2
drill

Step 1
Cut outer
shape

Step 2
drill

Bandsaw - 7°
Scrollsaw - 5°

68

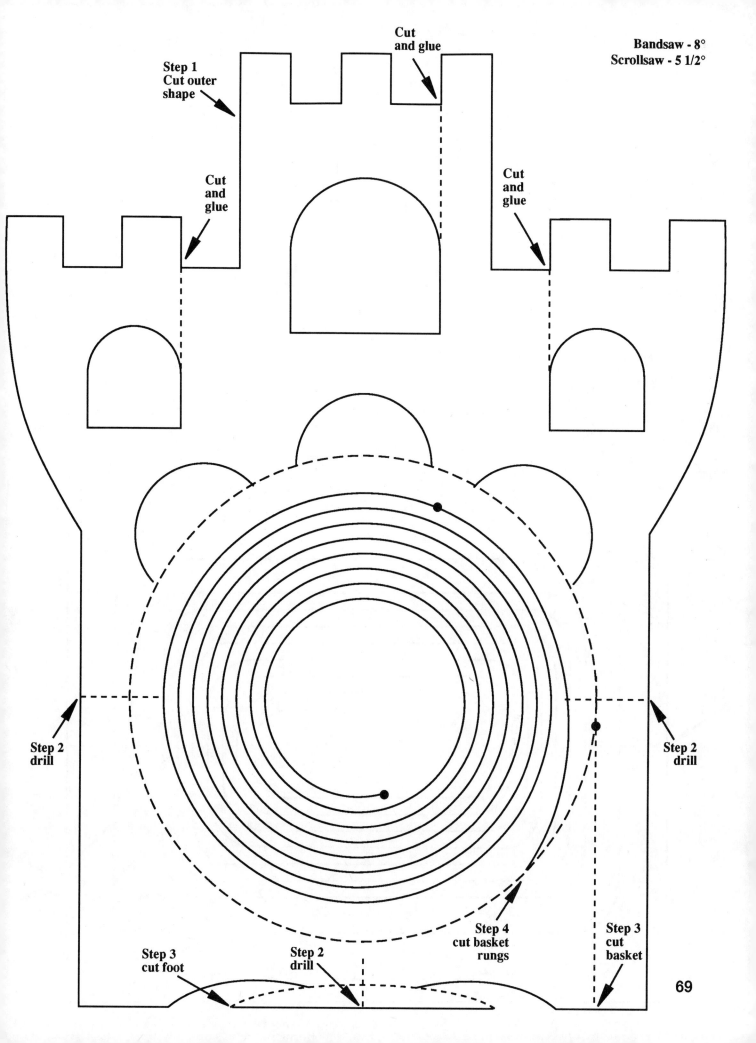

Step 1
Cut outer
shape

Cut
and glue

Bandsaw - 8°
Scrollsaw - 5 1/2°

Cut
and
glue

Cut
and
glue

Step 2
drill

Step 2
drill

Step 3
cut foot

Step 2
drill

Step 4
cut basket
rungs

Step 3
cut
basket

69

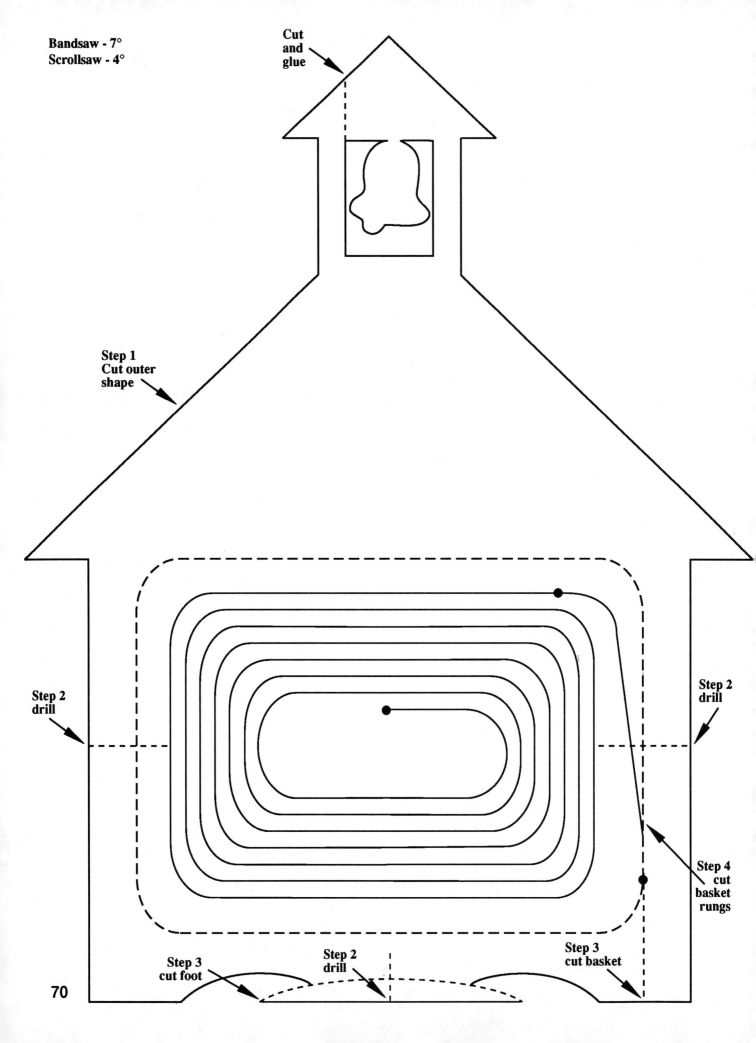

Bandsaw - 7°
Scrollsaw - 4°

Cut
and
glue

Step 1
Cut outer
shape

Step 2
drill

Step 2
drill

Step 4
cut
basket
rungs

Step 3
cut foot

Step 2
drill

Step 3
cut basket

70

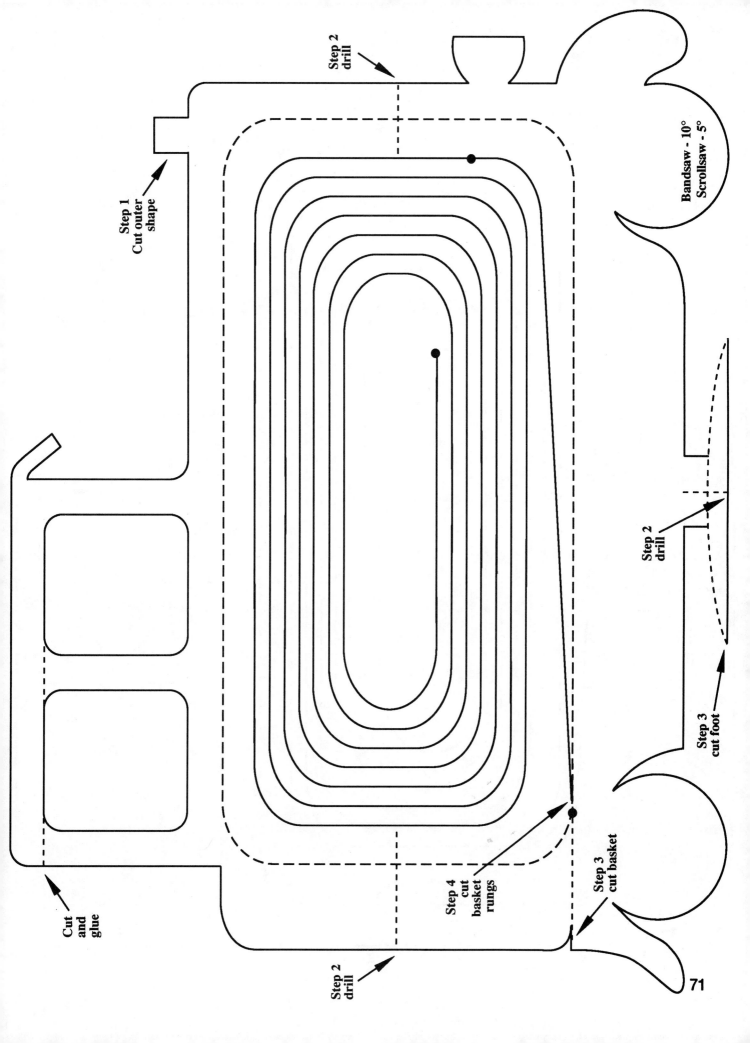

Step 2 drill

Step 1 Cut outer shape

Bandsaw - 10°
Scrollsaw - 5°

Step 2 drill

Step 3 cut foot

Cut and glue

Step 4 cut basket rungs

Step 3 cut basket

Step 2 drill

71

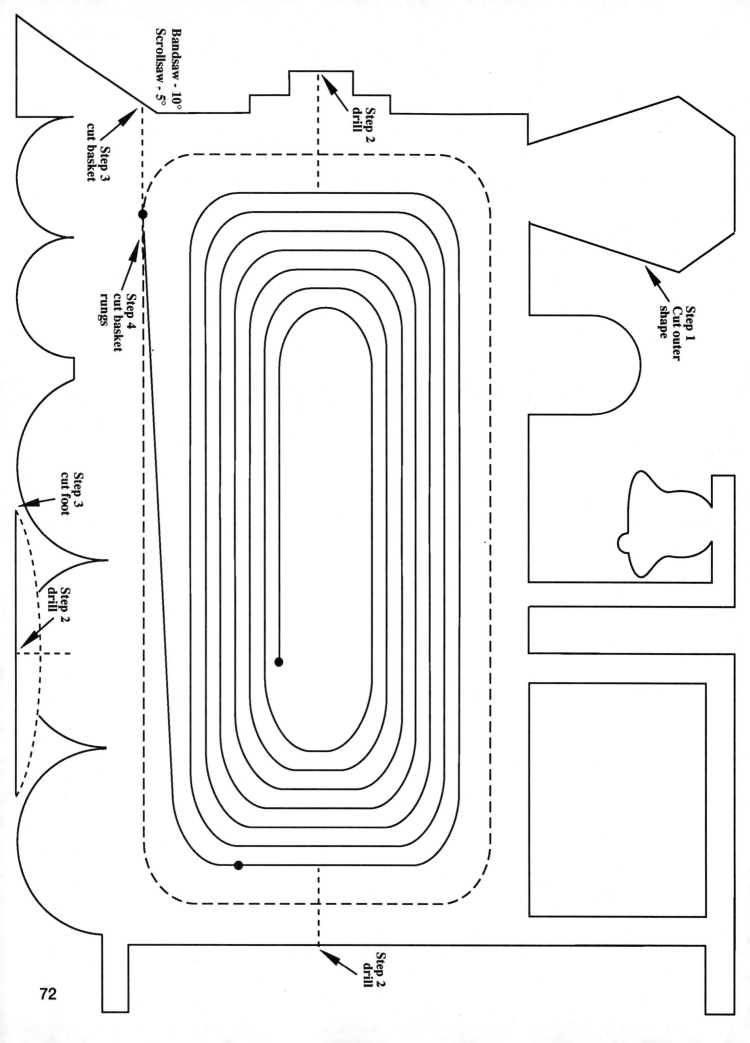

Bandsaw - 10°
Scrollsaw - 5°

Step 3
cut basket

Step 4
cut basket
rungs

Step 3
cut foot

Step 2
drill

Step 2
drill

Step 1
Cut outer
shape

Step 2
drill

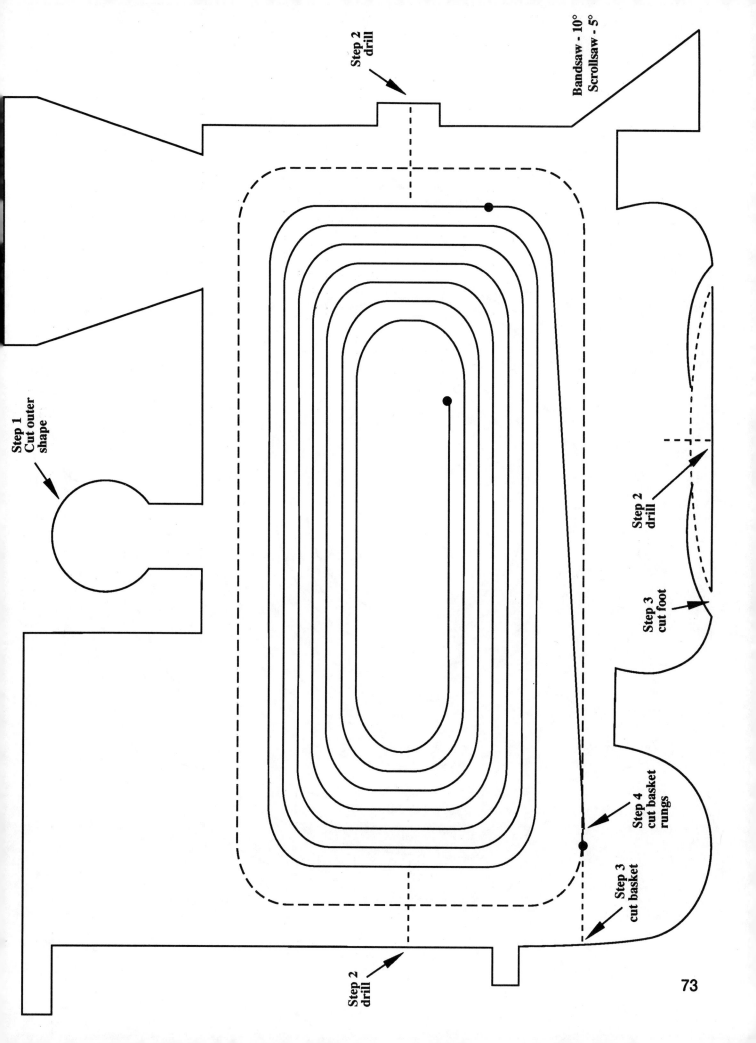

Bandsaw - 10°
Scrollsaw - 5°

Step 2
drill

Step 1
Cut outer
shape

Step 2
drill

Step 3
cut foot

Step 4
cut basket
rungs

Step 3
cut basket

Step 2
drill

Bandsaw - 7°
Scrollsaw - 5°

Step 2
drill

Step 1
Cut outer
shape

Step 3
cut basket

Step 3
Step 3
cut foot

Step 3
cut basket

Step 4
cut basket
rungs

Step 2
drill

Step 2
drill

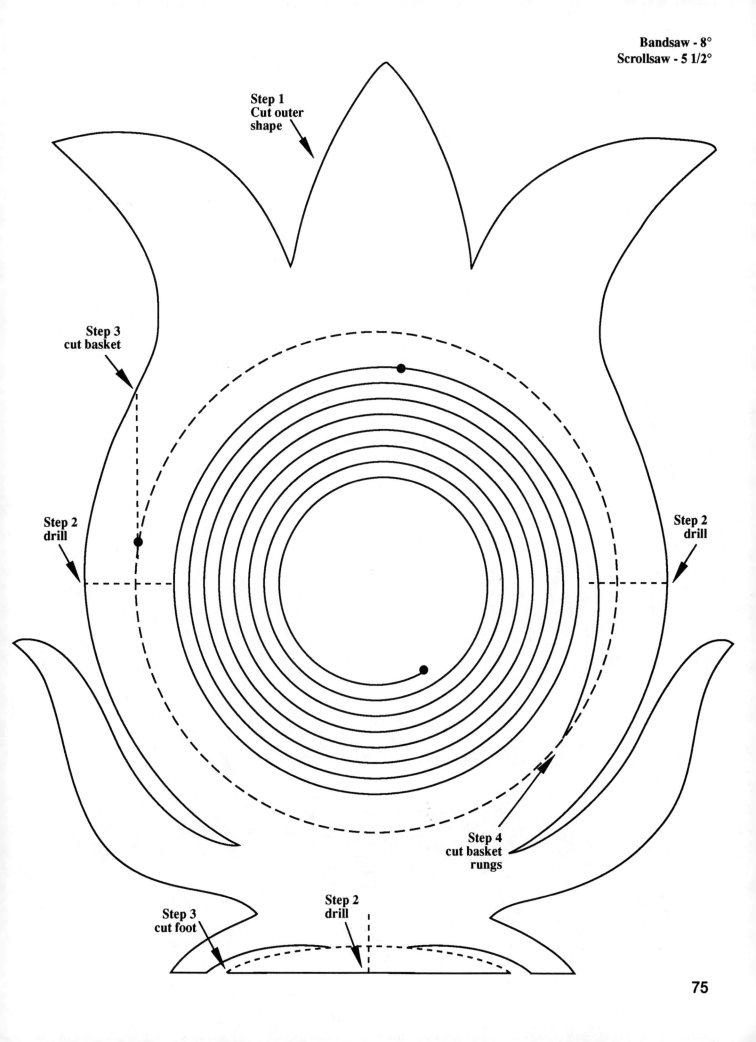

Bandsaw - 8°
Scrollsaw - 5 1/2°

Step 1
Cut outer
shape

Step 3
cut basket

Step 2
drill

Step 2
drill

Step 4
cut basket
rungs

Step 3
cut foot

Step 2
drill

75

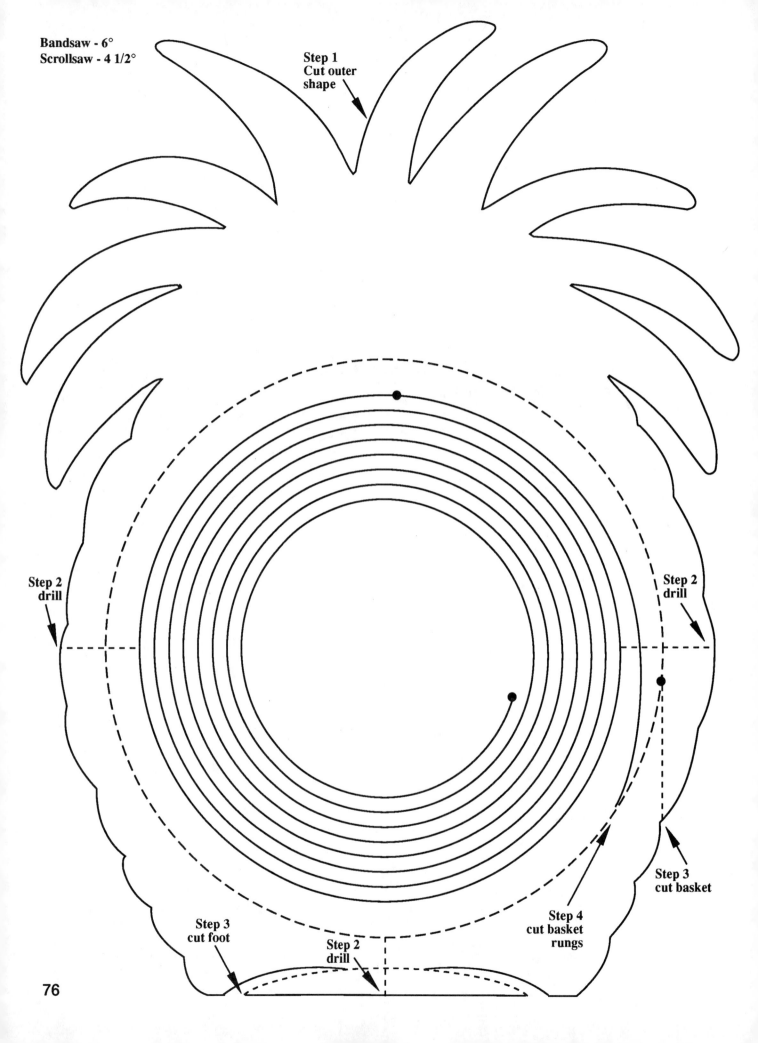

Bandsaw - 6°
Scrollsaw - 4 1/2°

Step 1
Cut outer
shape

Step 2
drill

Step 2
drill

Step 3
cut basket

Step 4
cut basket
rungs

Step 3
cut foot

Step 2
drill

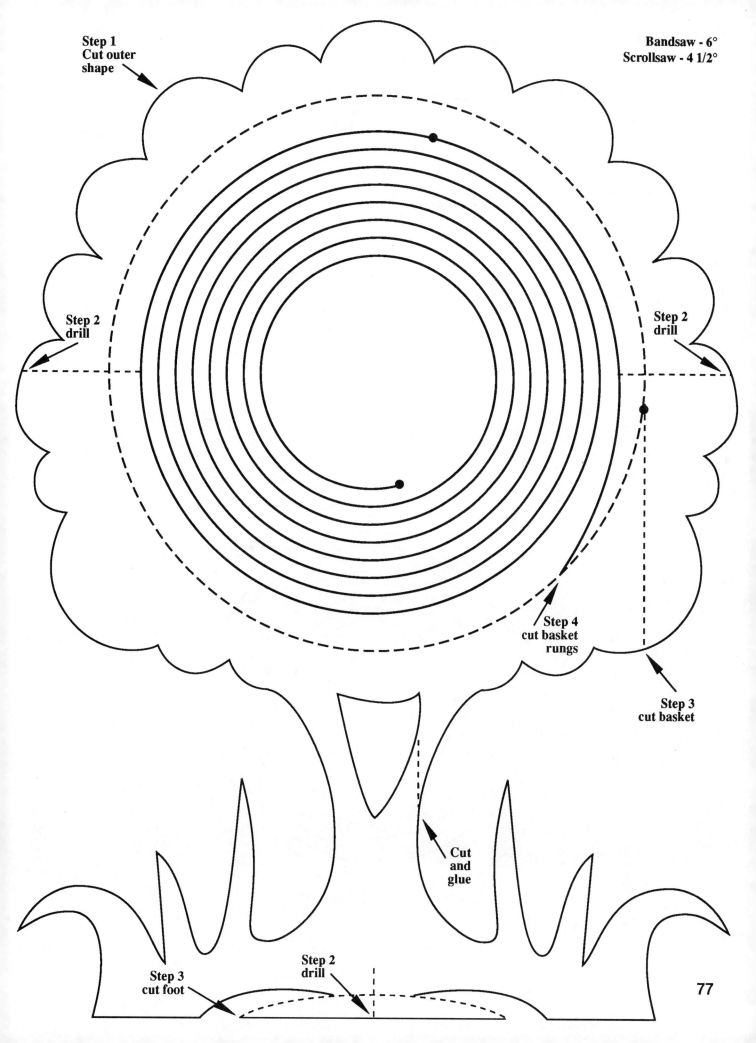

Step 1
Cut outer
shape

Bandsaw - 6°
Scrollsaw - 4 1/2°

Step 2
drill

Step 2
drill

Step 4
cut basket
rungs

Step 3
cut basket

Cut
and
glue

Step 3
cut foot

Step 2
drill

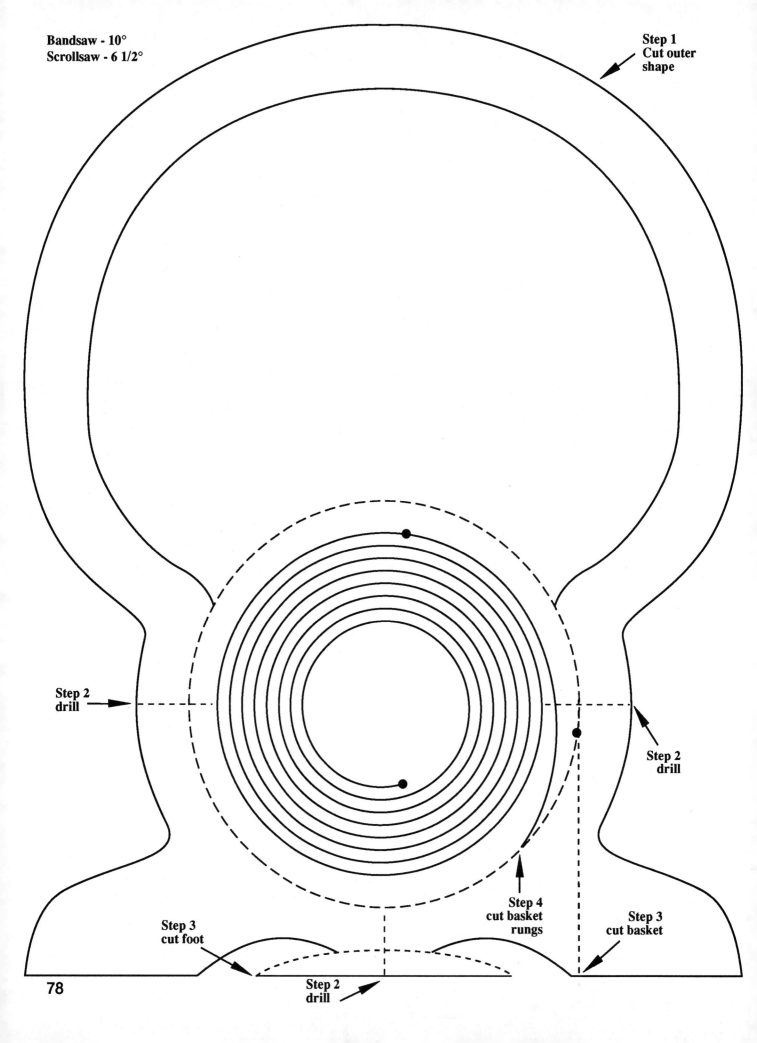

Bandsaw - 10°
Scrollsaw - 6 1/2°

Step 1
Cut outer
shape

Step 2
drill

Step 2
drill

Step 4
cut basket
rungs

Step 3
cut basket

Step 3
cut foot

Step 2
drill

78

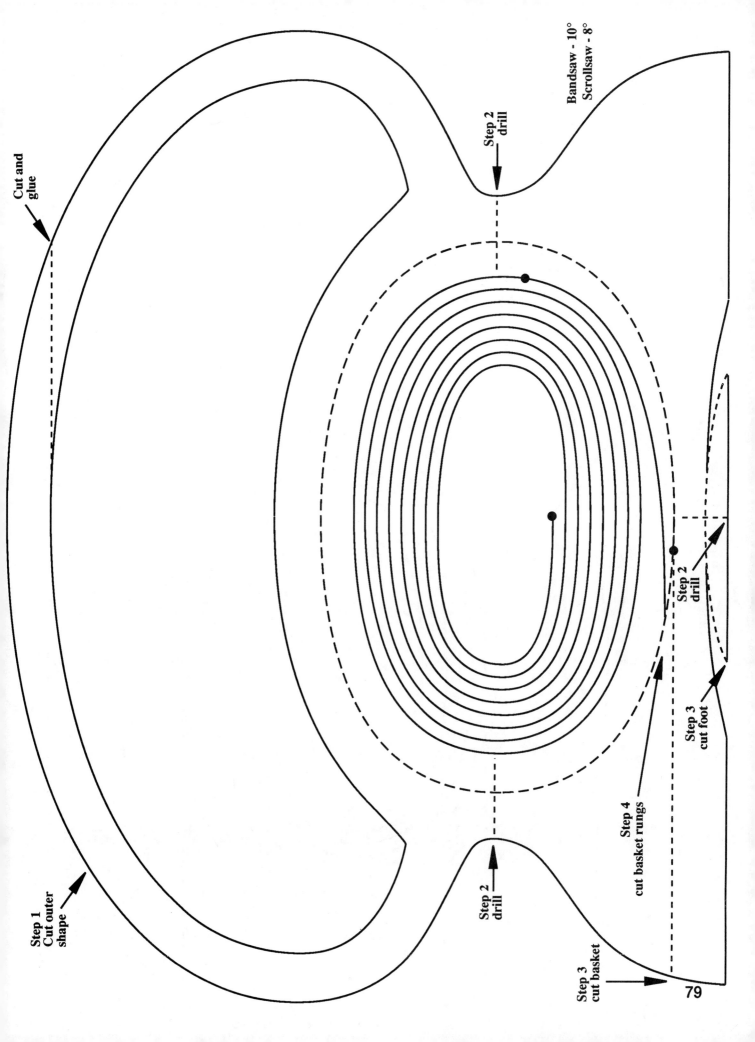

Cut and glue

Step 2 drill

Bandsaw - 10°
Scrollsaw - 8°

Step 1
Cut outer shape

Step 2 drill

Step 2 drill

Step 3
cut foot

Step 4
cut basket rungs

Step 3
cut basket

79

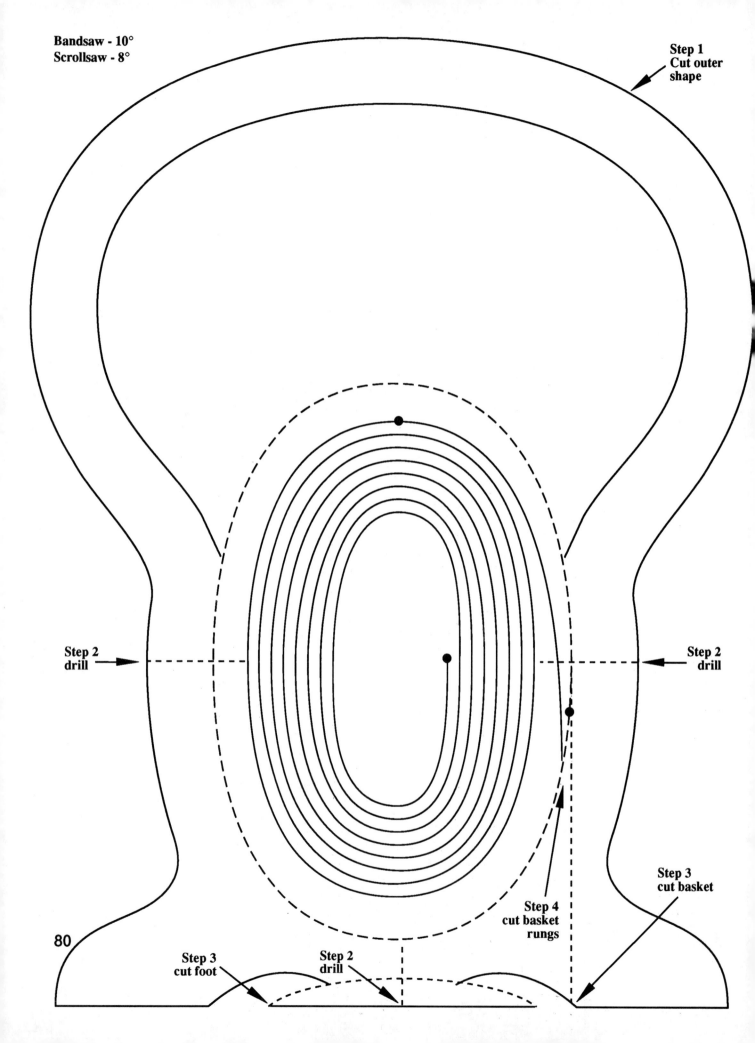

Bandsaw - 10°
Scrollsaw - 8°

Step 1
Cut outer
shape

Step 2
drill

Step 2
drill

80

Step 3
cut foot

Step 2
drill

Step 4
cut basket
rungs

Step 3
cut basket

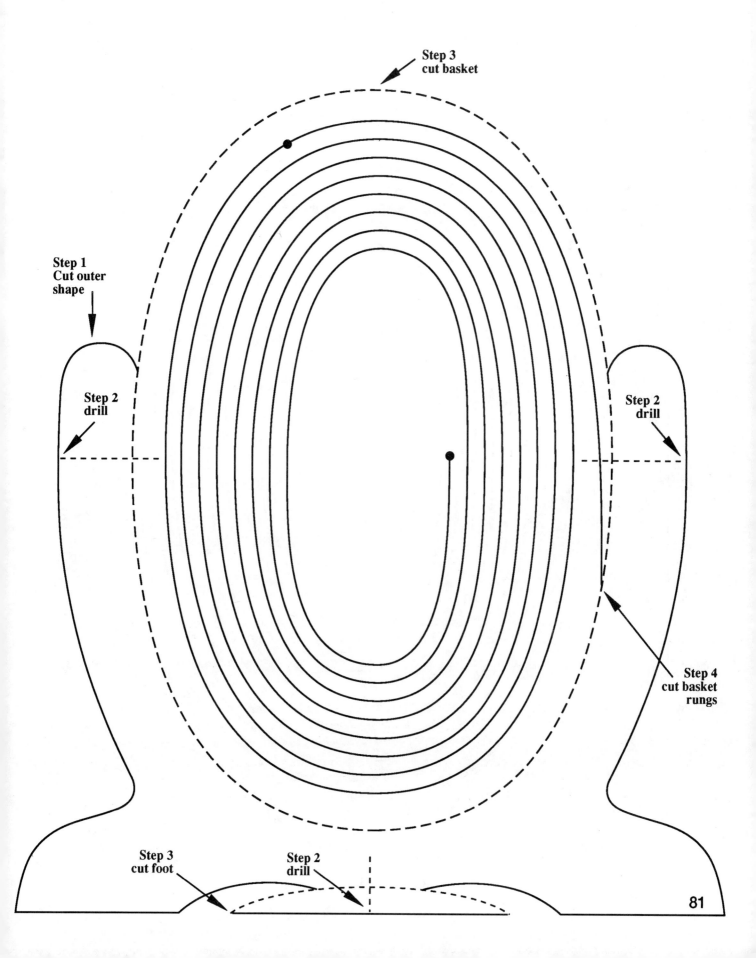

Bandsaw - 6°
Scrollsaw - 4°

Step 3
cut basket

Step 1
Cut outer
shape

Step 2
drill

Step 2
drill

Step 4
cut basket
rungs

Step 3
cut foot

Step 2
drill

81

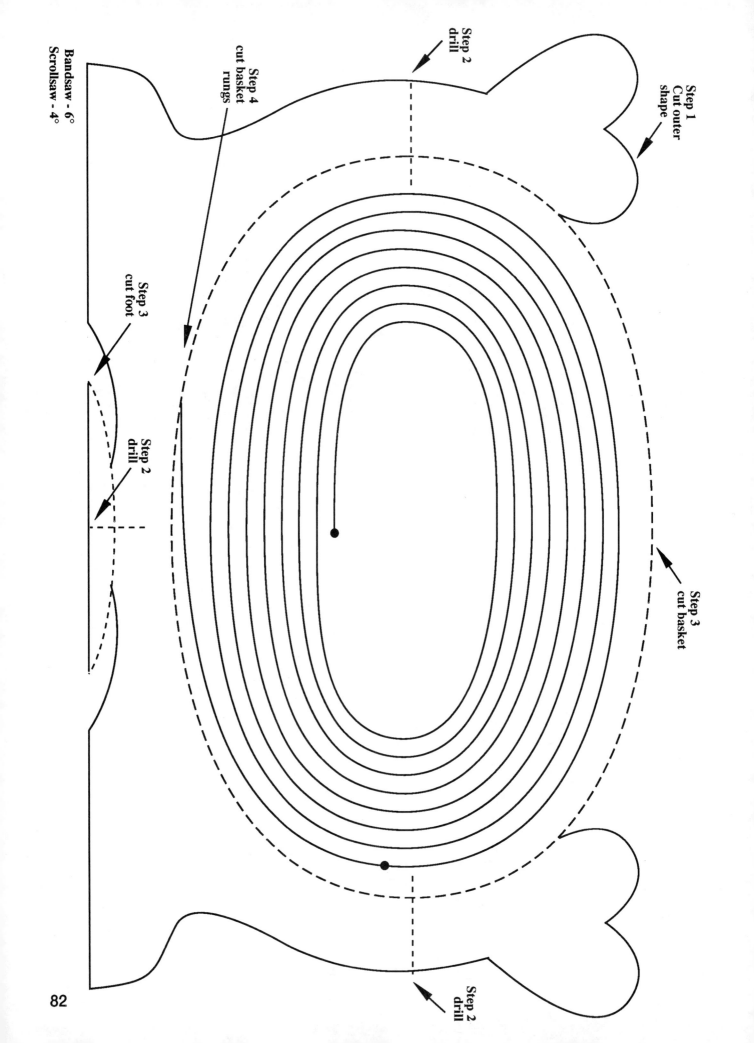

Step 1
Cut outer
shape

Step 2
drill

Step 3
cut basket

Step 4
cut basket
rungs

Step 3
cut foot

Step 2
drill

Step 2
drill

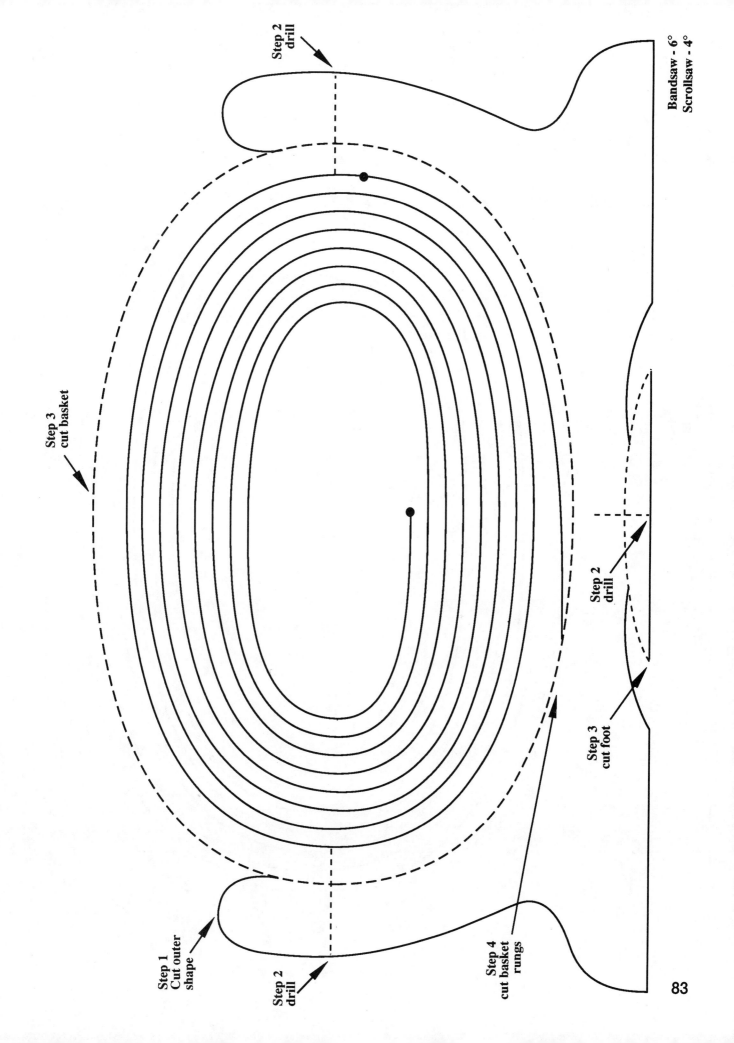

Step 2
drill

Bandsaw - 6°
Scrollsaw - 4°

Step 3
cut basket

Step 2
drill

Step 3
cut foot

Step 1
Cut outer
shape

Step 2
drill

Step 4
cut basket
rungs

83

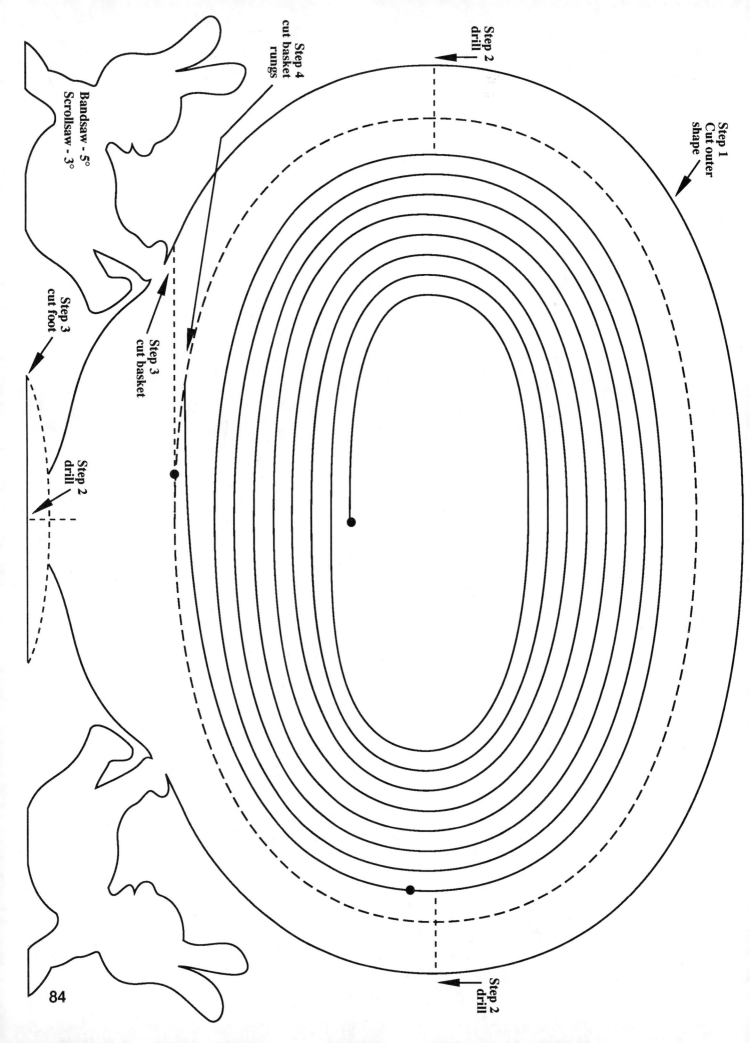

Step 1
Cut outer
shape

Step 2
drill

Step 2
drill

Step 4
cut basket
rungs

Step 3
cut basket

Step 3
cut basket

Step 3
cut foot

Step 2
drill

Bandsaw - 5°
Scrollsaw - 3°

84

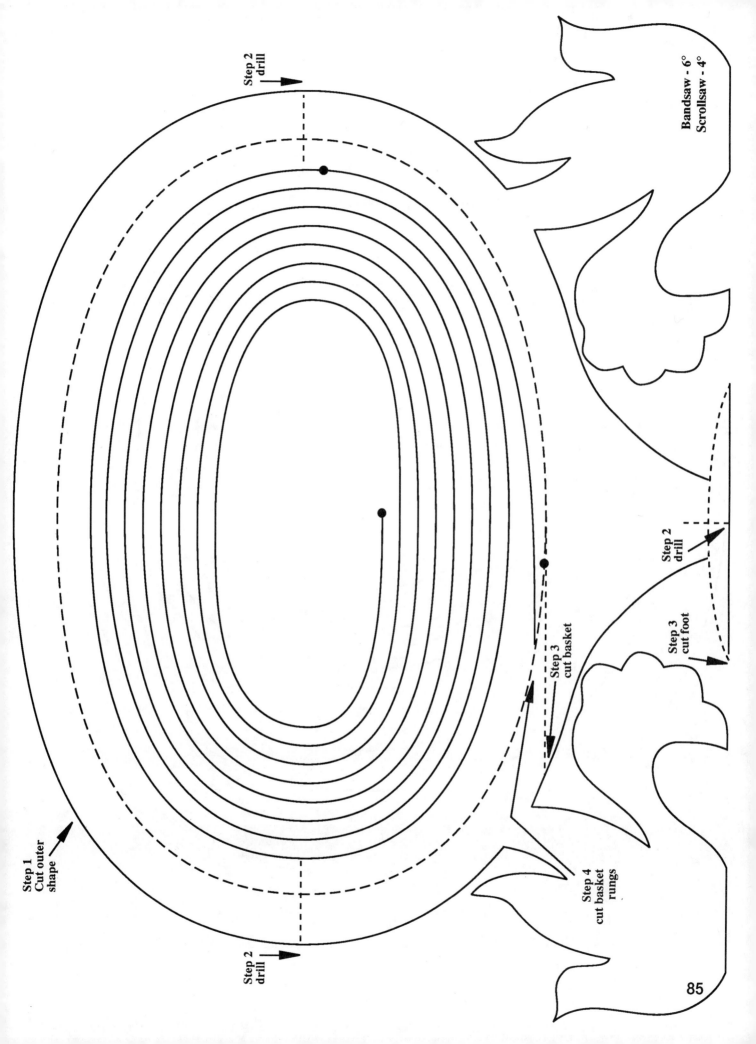

Step 2 drill

Step 1
Cut outer shape

Step 2 drill

Step 3
cut basket

Step 4
cut basket rungs

Step 2 drill

Step 3
cut foot

Bandsaw - 6°
Scrollsaw - 4°

85

Bandsaw - 5°
Scrollsaw - 4°

Step 3
cut basket

Step 1
Cut outer
shape

Step 2
drill

Step 2
drill

Step 4
cut basket
rungs

Step 3
cut foot

Step 2
drill

86

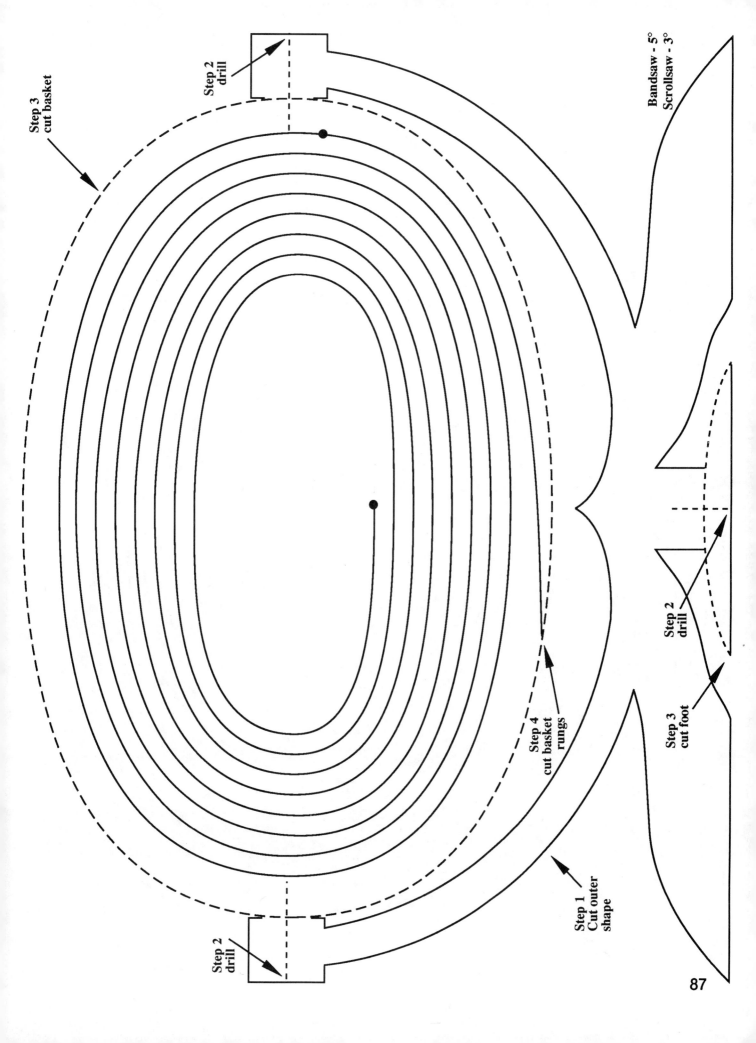

Step 3
cut basket

Step 2
drill

Bandsaw - 5°
Scrollsaw - 3°

Step 4
cut basket
rungs

Step 2
drill

Step 3
cut foot

Step 1
Cut outer
shape

Step 2
drill

87

Step 2
drill

Step 4
cut basket
rungs

Step 3
cut foot

Step 2
drill

Step 3
cut basket

Step 2
drill

Step 3
cut basket

Step 1
Cut outer
shape

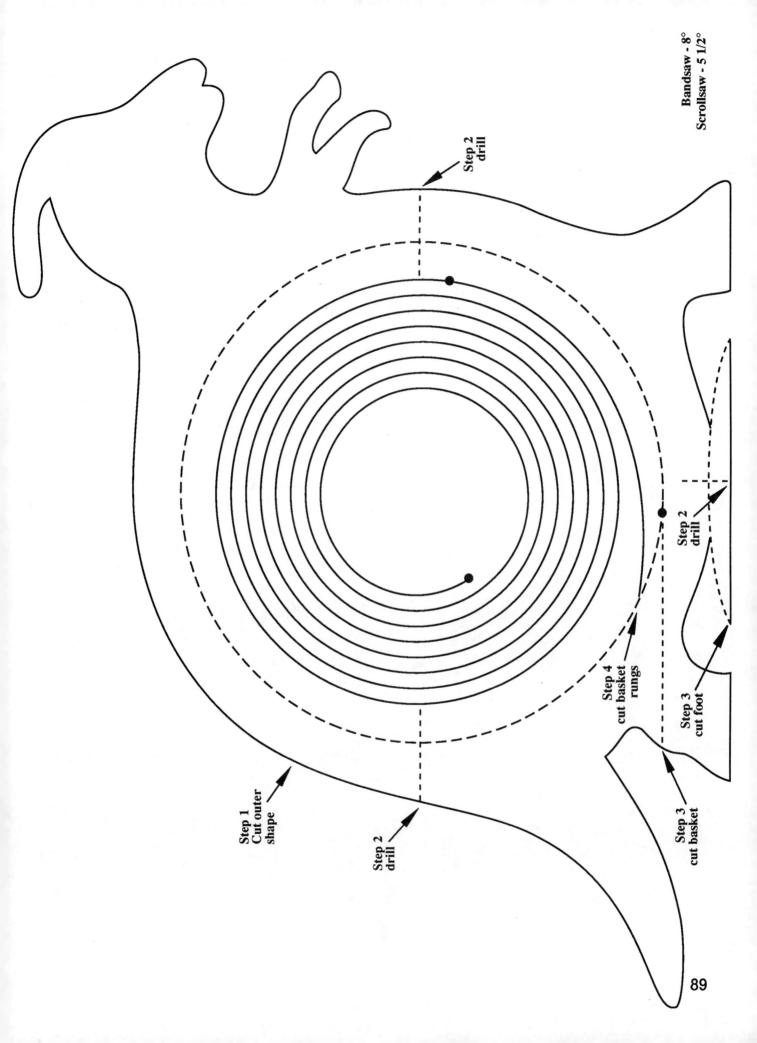

Step 2
drill

Bandsaw - 8°
Scrollsaw - 5 1/2°

Step 1
Cut outer
shape

Step 2
drill

Step 4
cut basket
rungs

Step 2
drill

Step 3
cut foot

Step 3
cut basket

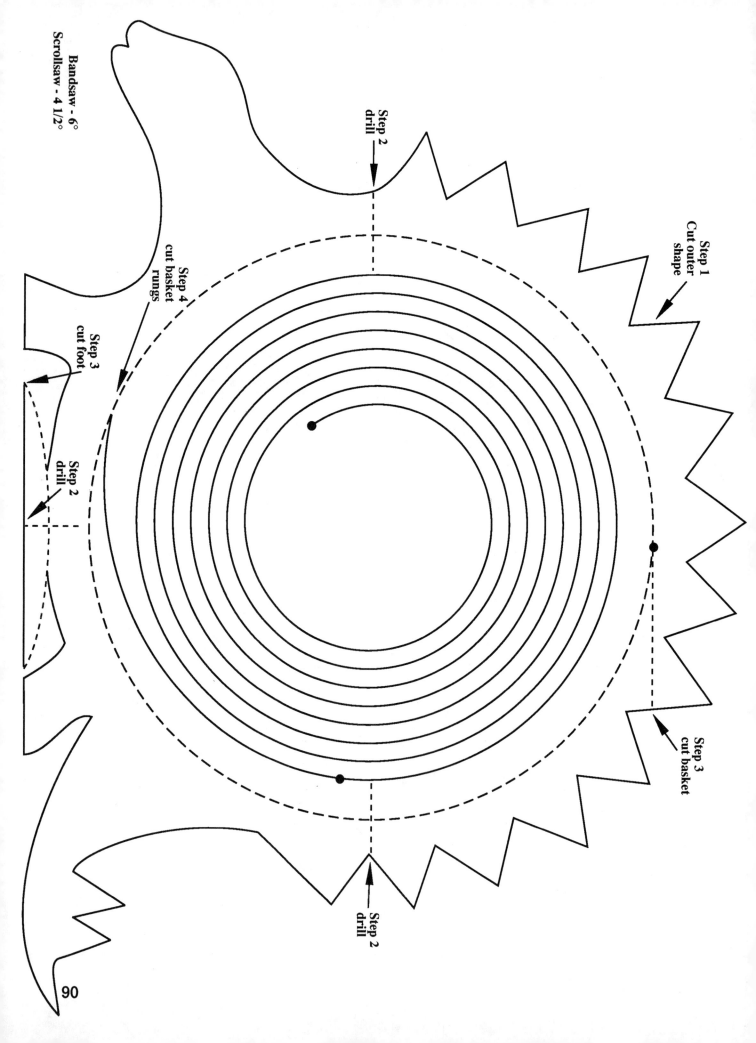

Bandsaw - 6°
Scrollsaw - 4 1/2°

Step 2
drill

Step 1
Cut outer
shape

Step 4
cut basket
rungs

Step 3
cut foot

Step 2
drill

Step 3
cut basket

Step 2
drill

90

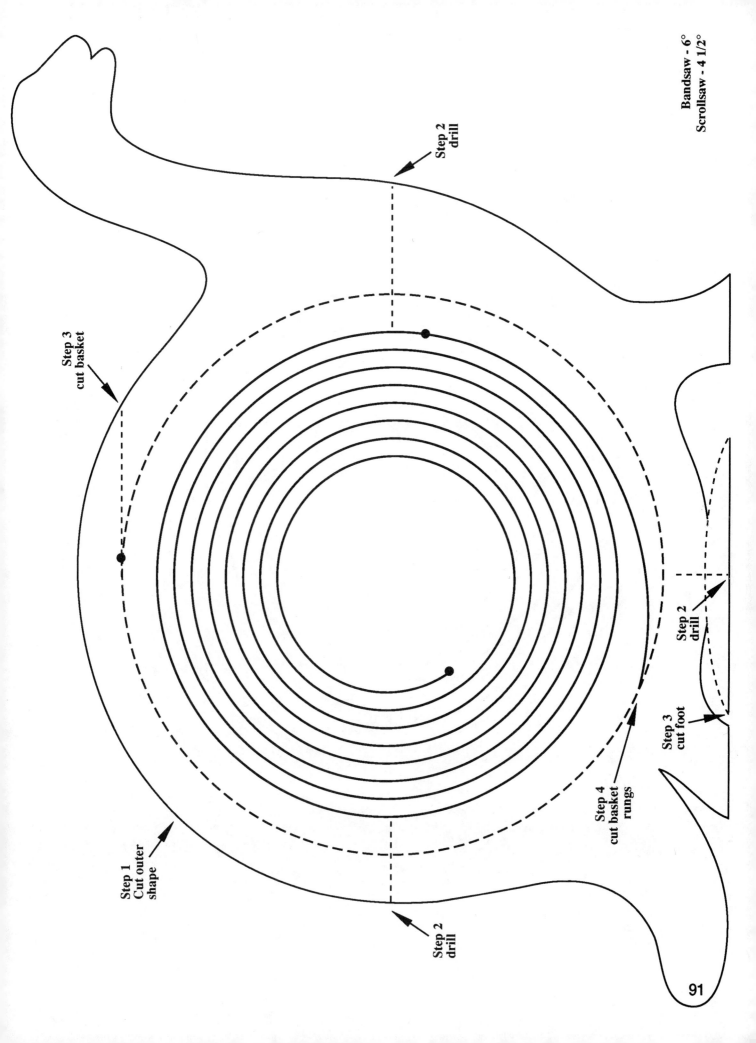

Step 2
drill

Bandsaw - 6°
Scrollsaw - 4 1/2°

Step 3
cut basket

Step 1
Cut outer
shape

Step 2
drill

Step 2
drill

Step 3
cut foot

Step 4
cut basket
rungs

91

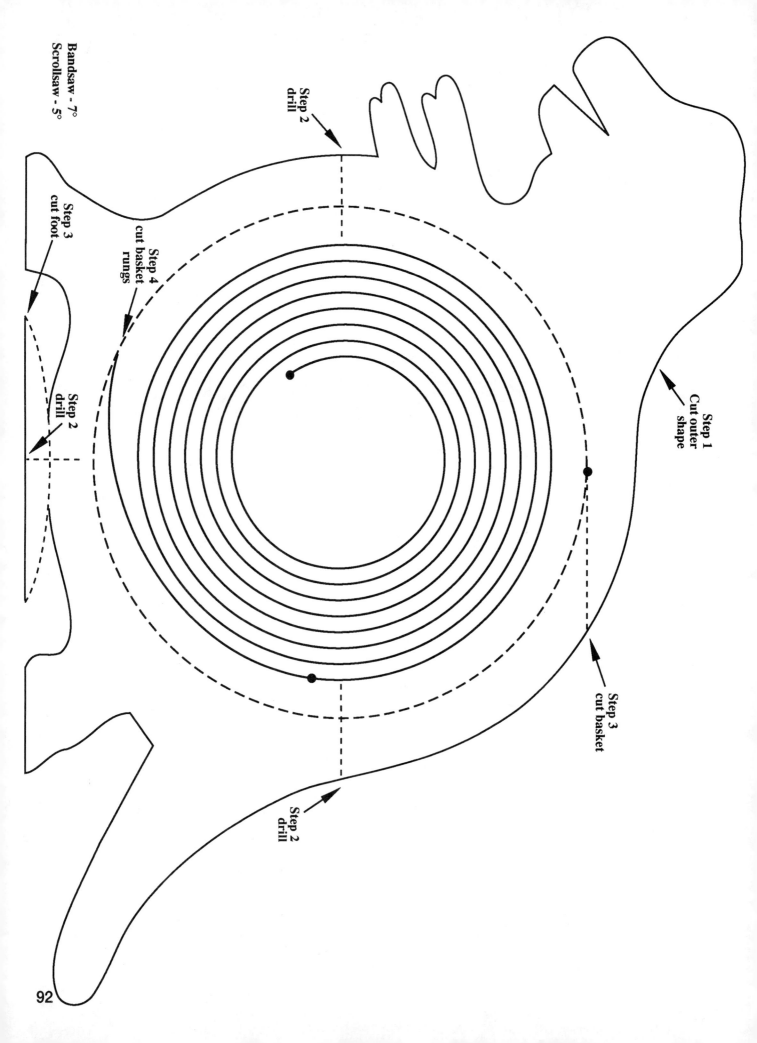

Bandsaw - 7°
Scrollsaw - 5°

Step 2
drill

Step 3
cut foot

Step 4
cut basket
rungs

Step 3
drill

Step 2
drill

Step 1
Cut outer
shape

Step 3
cut basket

Step 2
drill

1

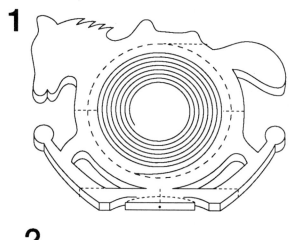

Bandsaw Instructions
For the Rocking Patterns

Step 1 Adhere pattern to work piece. Cut outer shape of basket.

Step 2 Mark the drill points using a hammer and center punch. Drill basket and foot pivot points the length of their dotted lines.

Step 3 Cut along dashed lines (with table flat) to separate inner basket and foot. Glue outer shape where cut was made, and clamp.

Step 4 Using the bevel indicated on the pattern, cut basket rungs following the solid line, shut off saw and back out blade. Glue 1"-2" at start of cut, and clamp.

Step 5 Assemble basket and foot with screws at drilled pivot points.

2

Drill ➤   ◄ Drill

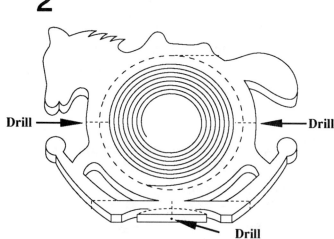

Drill

3

Clamp

Cut and glue

Clamp

Cut and glue

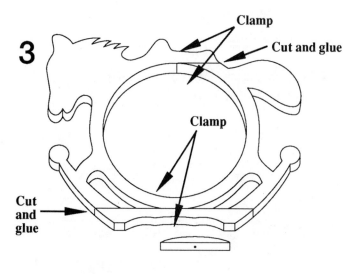

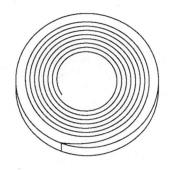

4

Clamp

Glue ➤

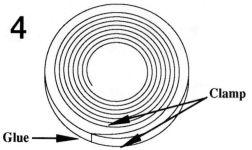

5

θ

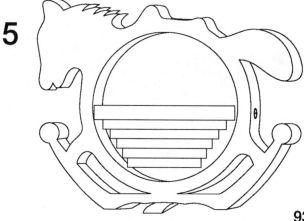

1

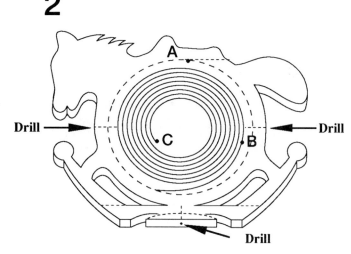

Scrollsaw Instructions
For the Rocking Patterns

Step 1 Adhere pattern to work piece. Cut outer shape of basket.

Step 2 Mark the drill points using a hammer and center punch. Drill basket and foot pivot points the length of their dotted lines.

2

Drill →

← Drill

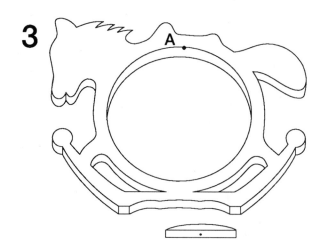

Drill

Step 3 With table flat, cut along dashed lines to separate foot. Drill at points A, B, C using a 1/16" drill bit. Beginning at Point A, cut along dashed lines (with table flat) to separate inner basket from the outer shape.

Step 4 Using the bevel indicated on the pattern, cut basket rungs following the solid line. If your table tilts to the left begin your cut at Point C and finish at Point B. If your table tilts to the right begin your cut at Point B and finish at Point C. **Note**: It is easier to begin at Point C and end at Point B.

Step 5 Assemble basket and foot with screws at drilled pivot points.

3

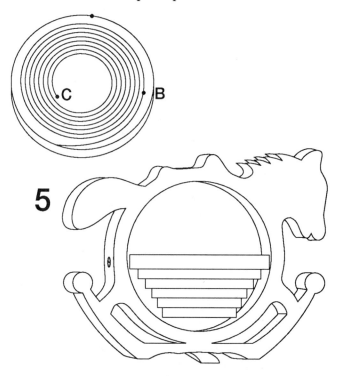

4

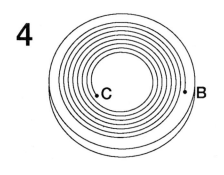

5

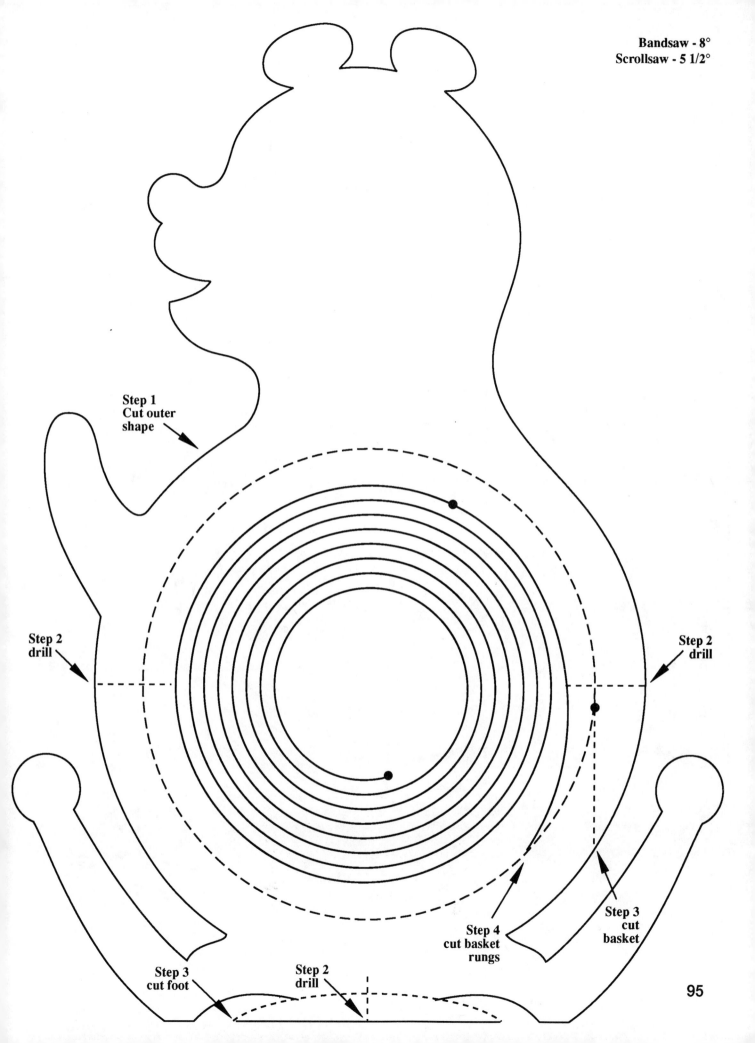

Bandsaw - 8°
Scrollsaw - 5 1/2°

Step 1
Cut outer
shape

Step 2
drill

Step 2
drill

Step 3
cut foot

Step 2
drill

Step 4
cut basket
rungs

Step 3
cut
basket

95

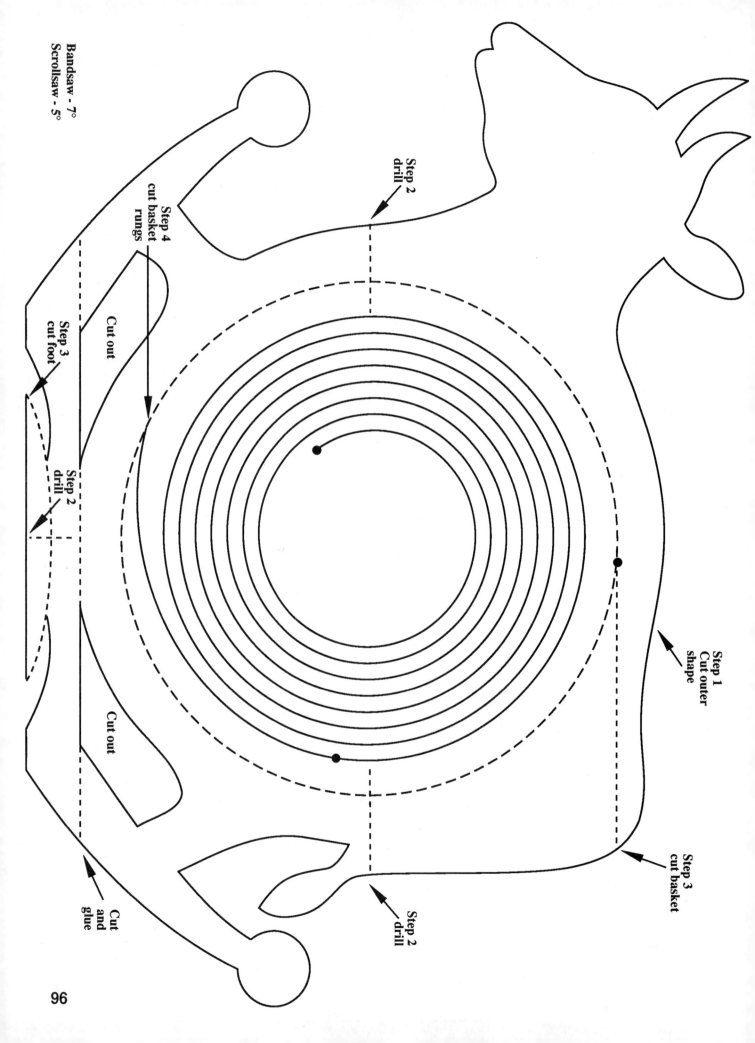

Scrollsaw - 5°

Step 4
cut basket
rungs

Step 3
cut foot

Cut out

Step 2
drill

Cut out

Cut
and
glue

Step 2
drill

Step 1
Cut outer
shape

Step 3
cut basket

Step 2
drill

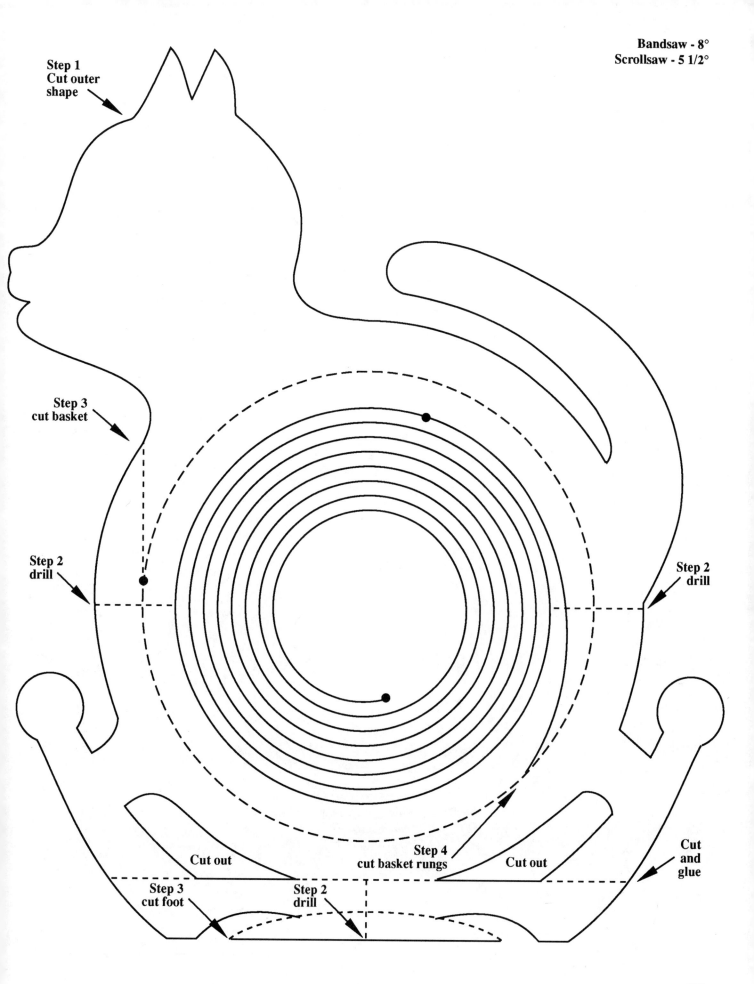

Bandsaw - 8°
Scrollsaw - 5 1/2°

Step 1
Cut outer
shape

Step 3
cut basket

Step 2
drill

Step 2
drill

Step 4
cut basket rungs

Cut out

Cut out

Cut
and
glue

Step 3
cut foot

Step 2
drill

97

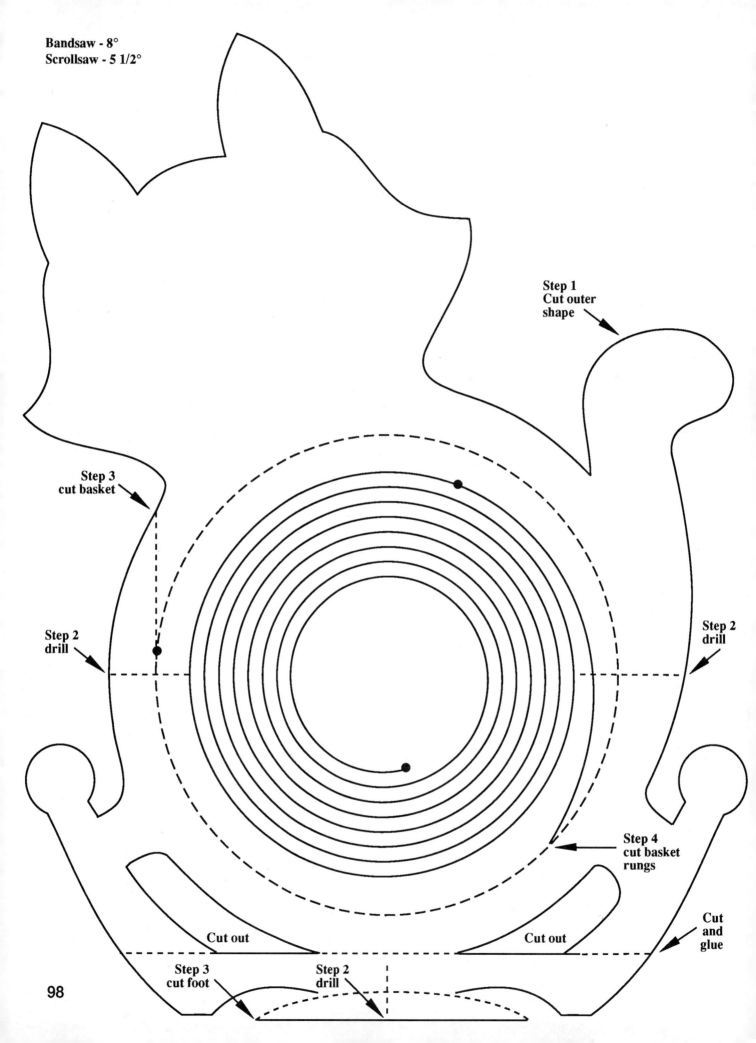

Bandsaw - 8°
Scrollsaw - 5 1/2°

Step 1
Cut outer
shape

Step 3
cut basket

Step 2
drill

Step 2
drill

Step 4
cut basket
rungs

Cut
and
glue

Cut out

Cut out

Step 3
cut foot

Step 2
drill

98

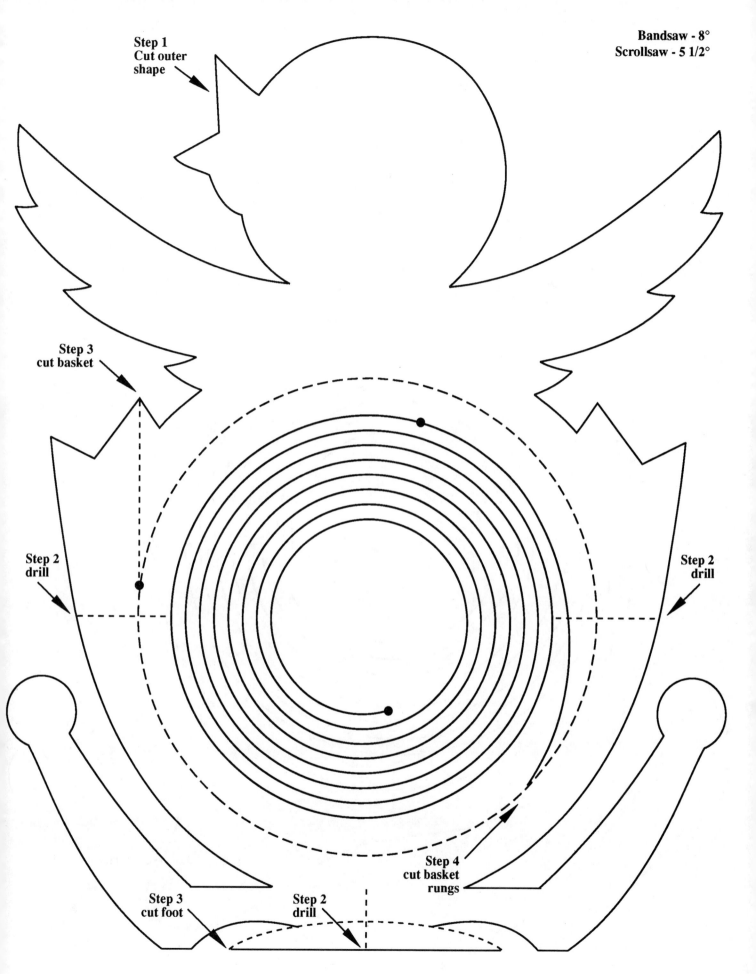

Bandsaw - 8°
Scrollsaw - 5 1/2°

Step 1
Cut outer
shape

Step 3
cut basket

Step 2
drill

Step 2
drill

Step 4
cut basket
rungs

Step 3
cut foot

Step 2
drill

99

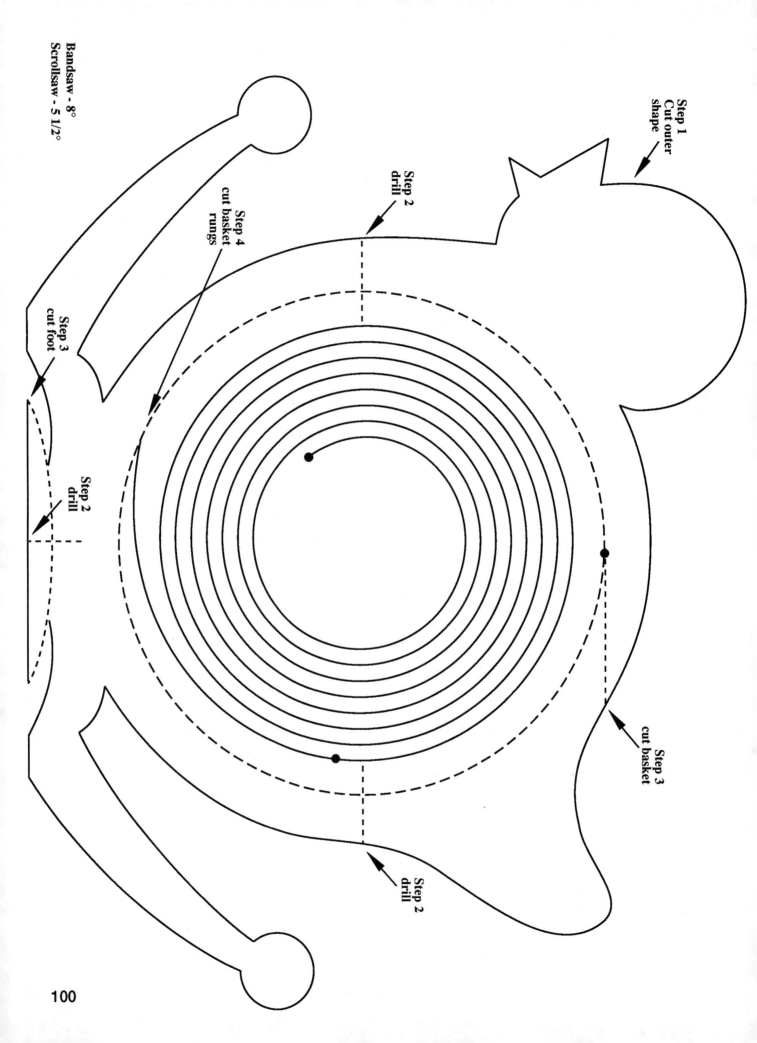

Step 1
Cut outer
shape

Step 2
drill

Step 4
cut basket
rungs

Step 3
cut foot

Step 2
drill

Step 3
cut basket

Step 2
drill

Bandsaw - 8°
Scrollsaw - 5 1/2°

100

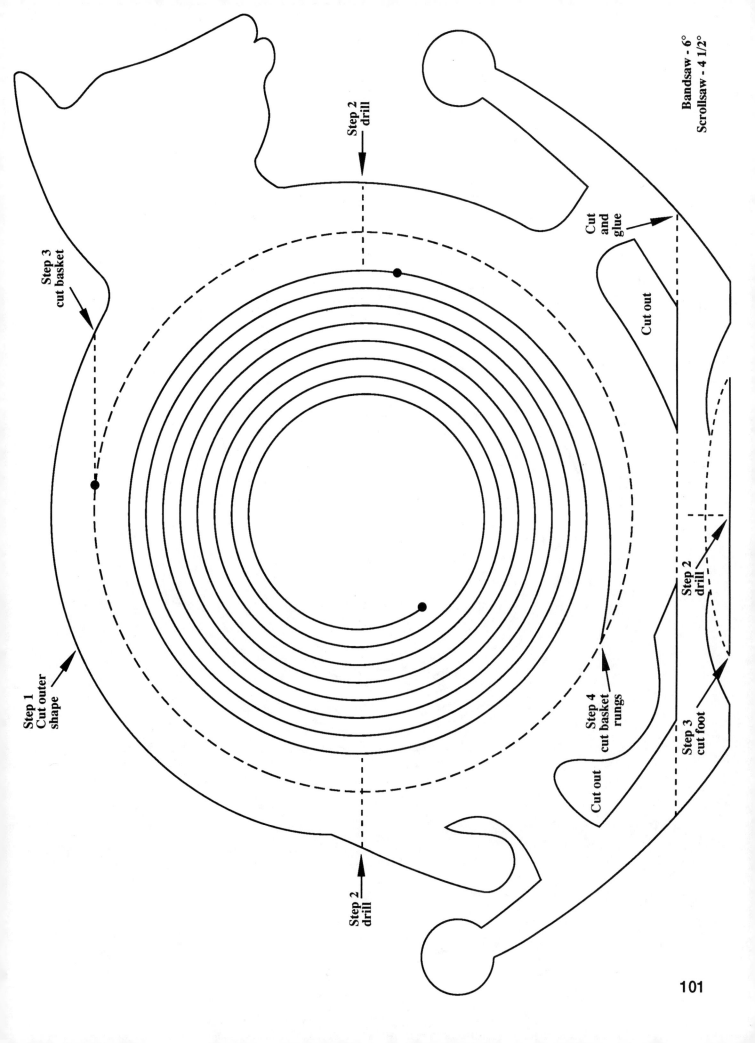

Step 3
cut basket

Step 2
drill

Bandsaw - 6°
Scrollsaw - 4 1/2°

Cut
and
glue

Cut out

Step 1
Cut outer
shape

Step 4
cut basket
rungs

Step 2
drill

Cut out

Step 3
cut foot

Step 2
drill

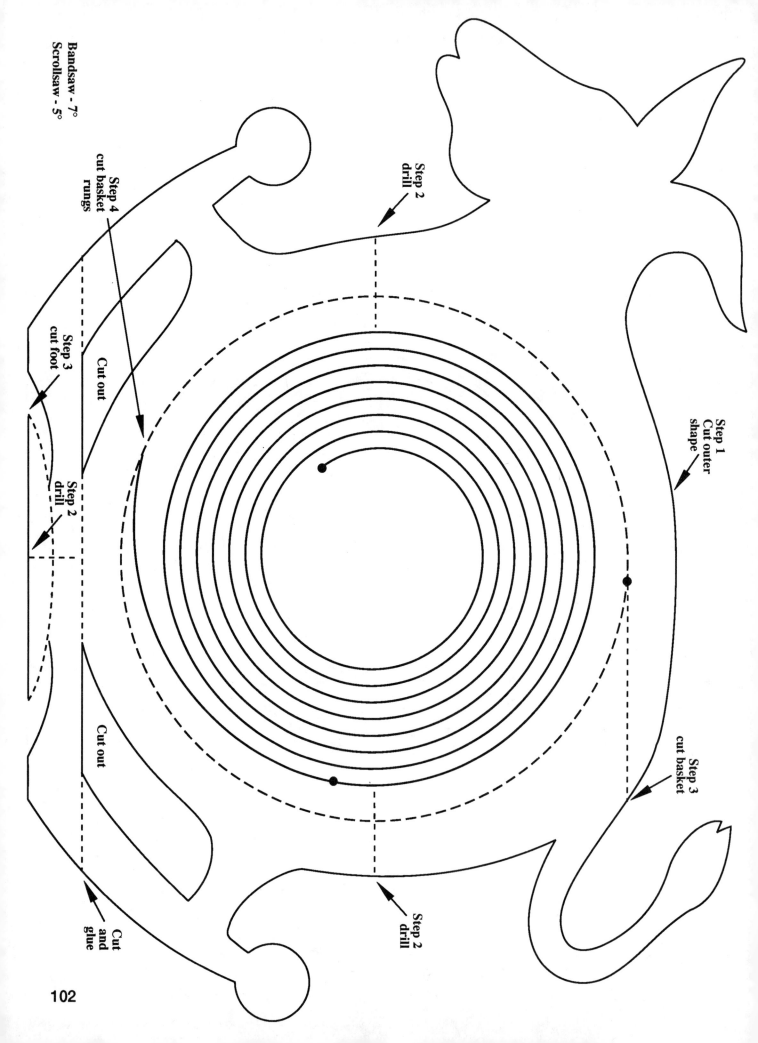

Bandsaw - 7°
Scrollsaw - 5°

Step 4
cut basket
rungs

Step 3
cut foot

Step 2
drill

Cut
and
glue

Step 2
drill

Cut out

Step 2
drill

Cut out

Step 1
Cut outer
shape

Step 3
cut basket

102

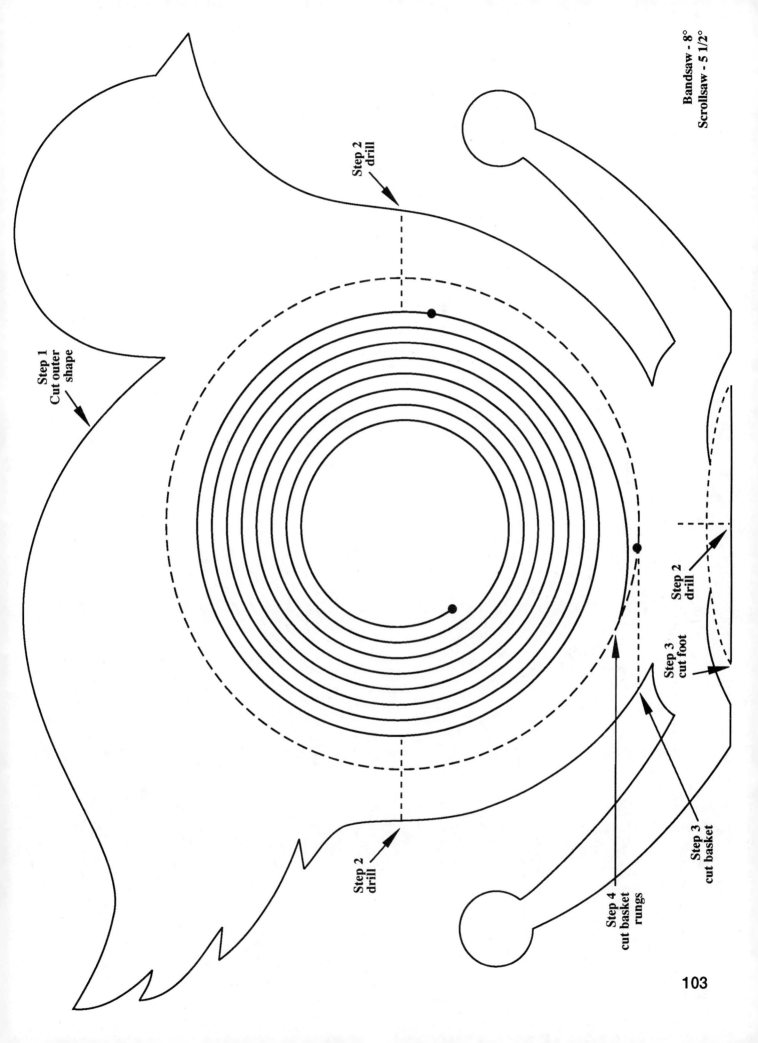

Step 1
Cut outer shape

Step 2
drill

Step 2
drill

Step 2
drill

Step 3
cut foot

Step 3
cut basket

Step 4
cut basket
rungs

Bandsaw - 8°
Scrollsaw - 5 1/2°

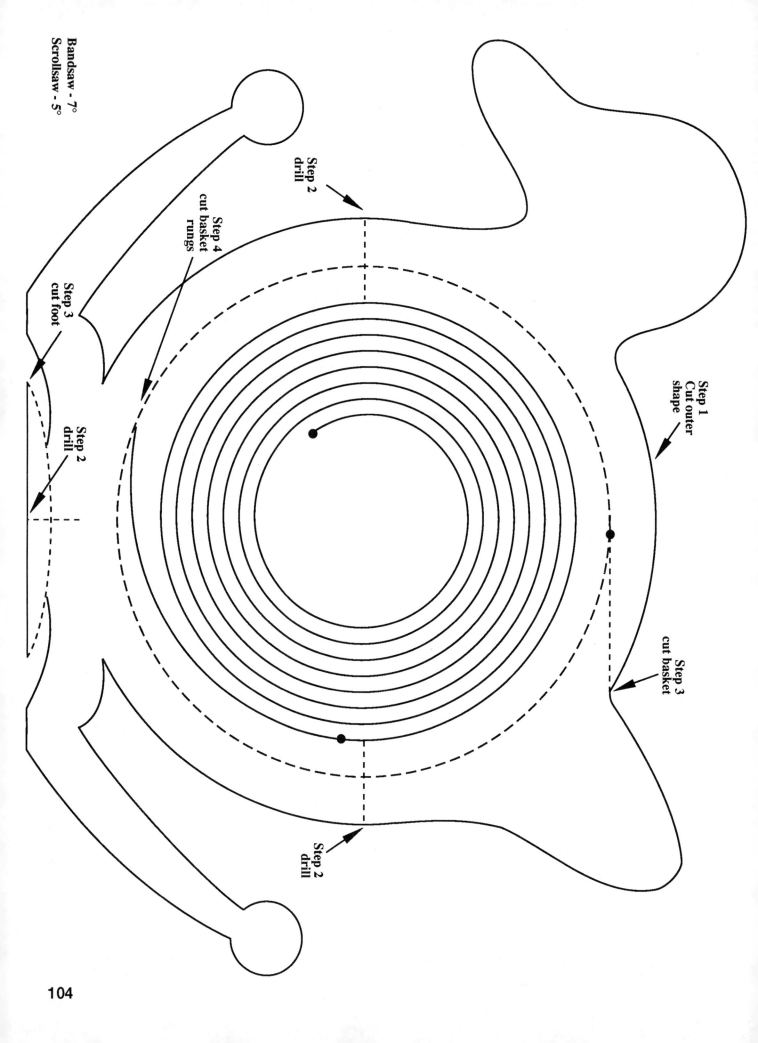

Bandsaw - 7°
Scrollsaw - 5°

Step 2
drill

Step 4
cut basket
rungs

Step 3
cut foot

Step 2
drill

Step 1
Cut outer
shape

Step 3
cut basket

Step 2
drill

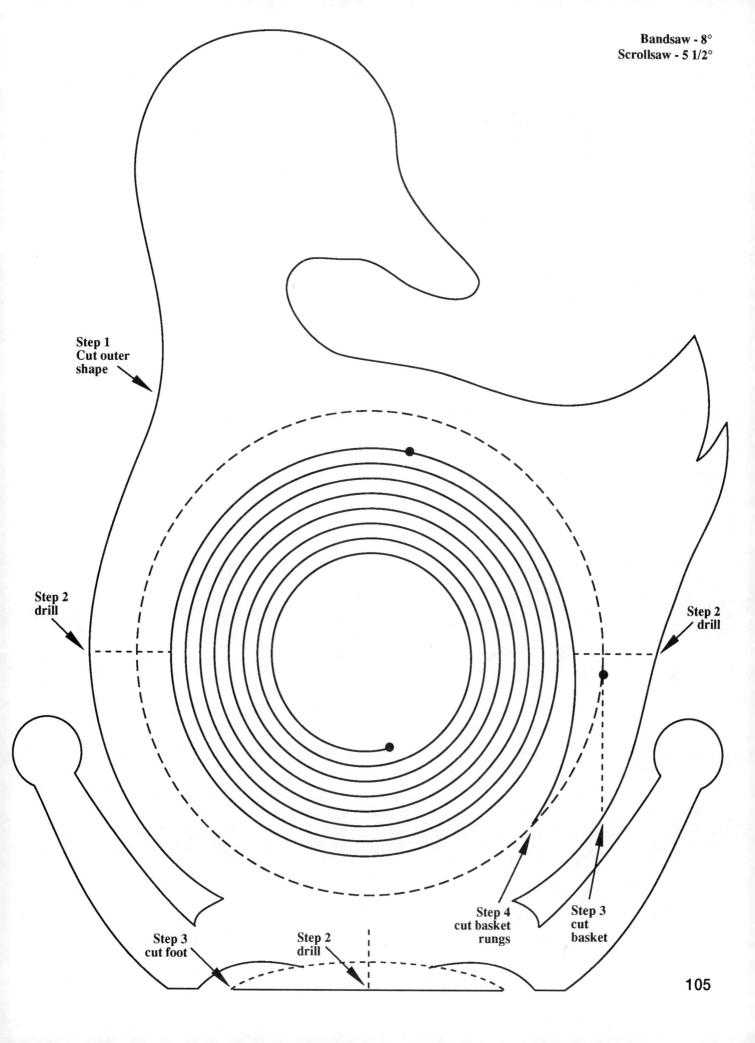

Bandsaw - 8°
Scrollsaw - 5 1/2°

Step 1
Cut outer
shape

Step 2
drill

Step 2
drill

Step 4
cut basket
rungs

Step 3
cut
basket

Step 3
cut foot

Step 2
drill

105

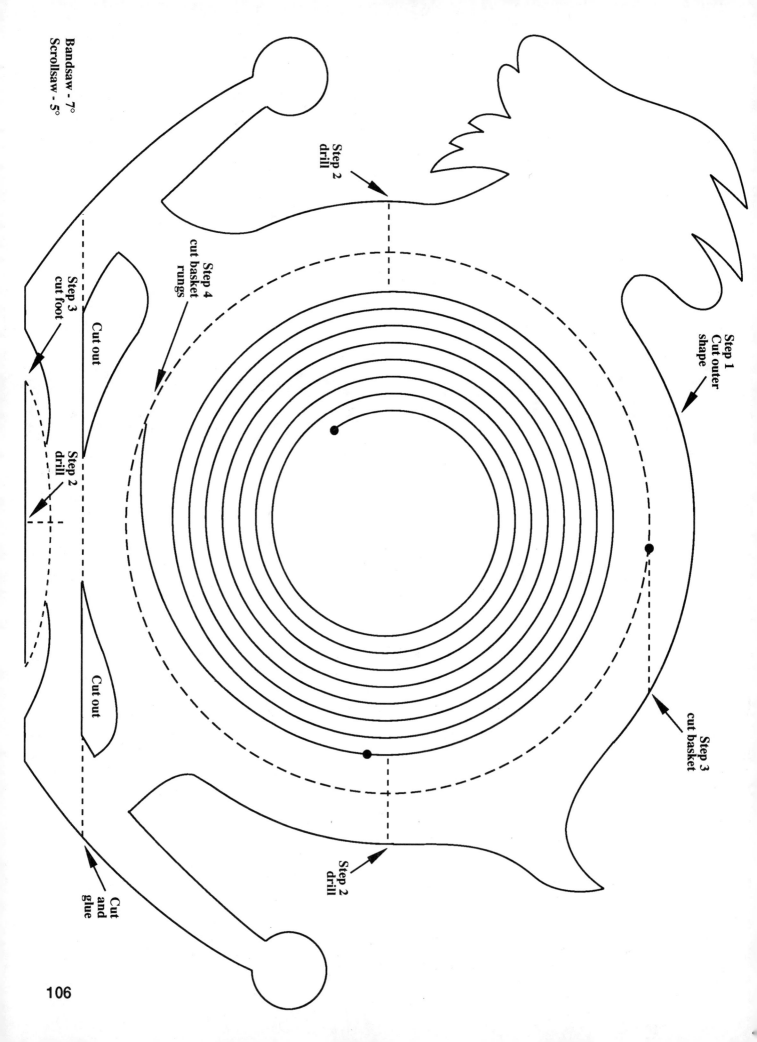

Bandsaw - 7°
Scrollsaw - 5°

Step 2
drill

Step 4
cut basket
rungs

Step 3
cut foot

Cut out

Step 2
drill

Step 1
Cut outer
shape

Step 3
cut basket

Cut out

Step 2
drill

Cut
and
glue

106

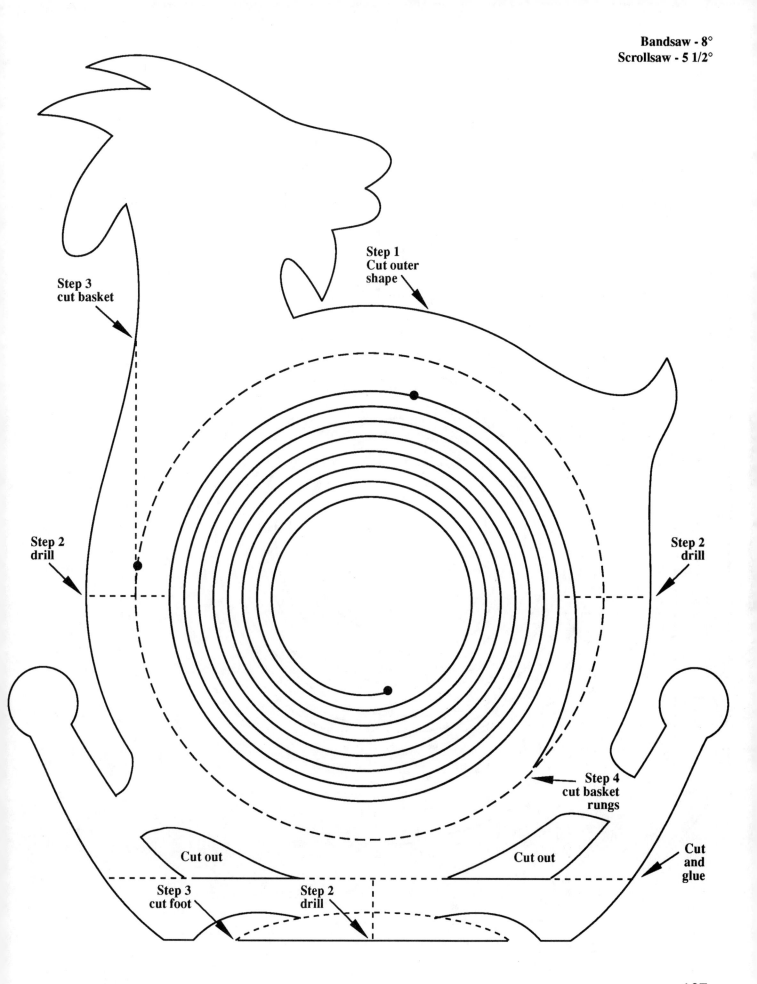

Bandsaw - 8°
Scrollsaw - 5 1/2°

Step 1
Cut outer
shape

Step 3
cut basket

Step 2
drill

Step 2
drill

Step 4
cut basket
rungs

Cut out

Cut out

Cut
and
glue

Step 3
cut foot

Step 2
drill

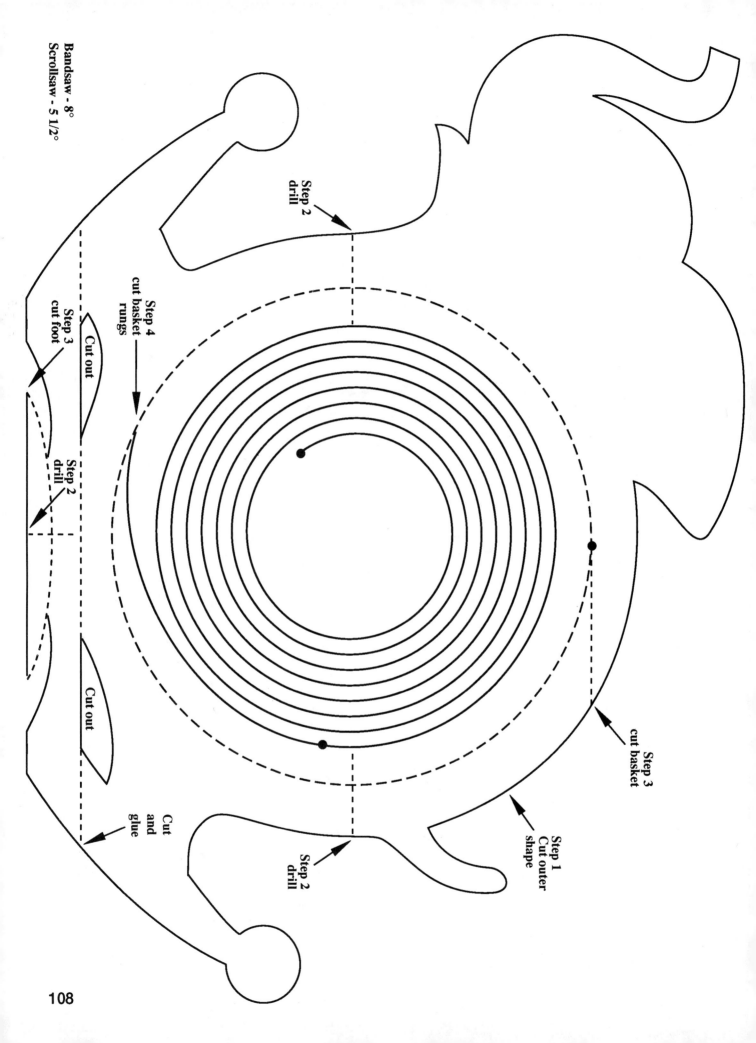

Bandsaw - 8°
Scrollsaw - 5 1/2°

Step 2
drill

Step 4
cut basket
rungs

Step 3
cut foot

Cut out

Step 3
Step 2
drill

Cut out

Step 3
cut basket

Step 1
Cut outer
shape

Cut
and
glue

Step 2
drill

108

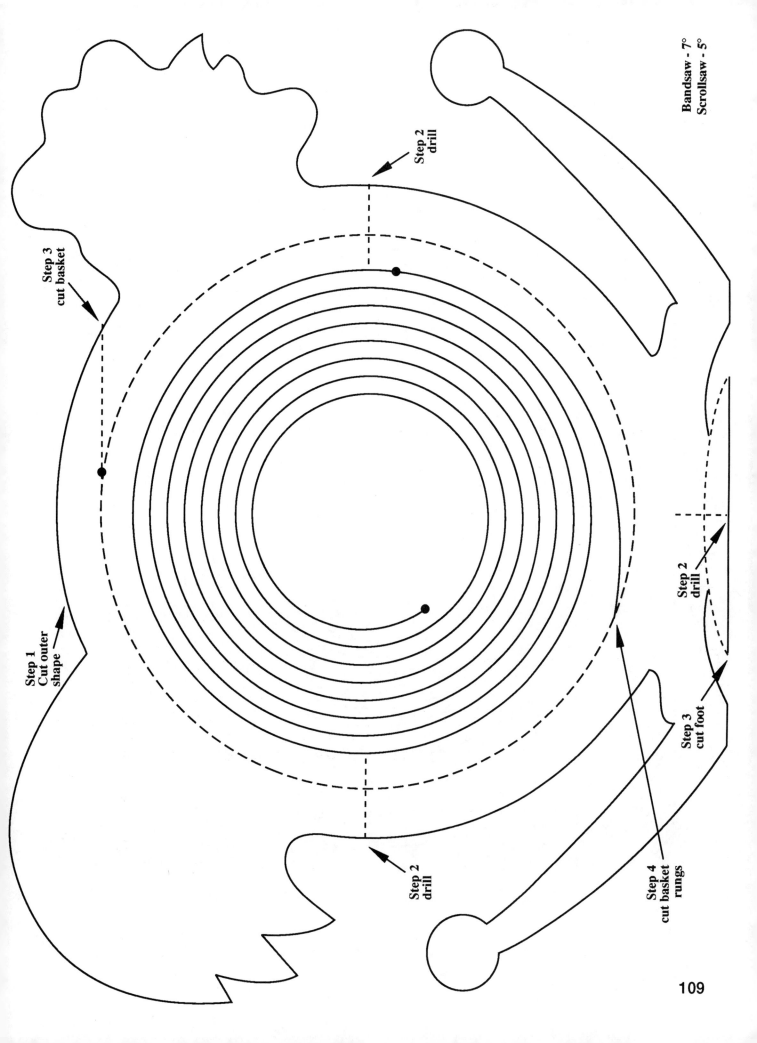

Step 3
cut basket

Step 2
drill

Step 1
Cut outer
shape

Step 2
drill

Step 2
drill

Step 3
cut foot

Step 4
cut basket
rungs

Bandsaw - 7°
Scrollsaw - 5°

109

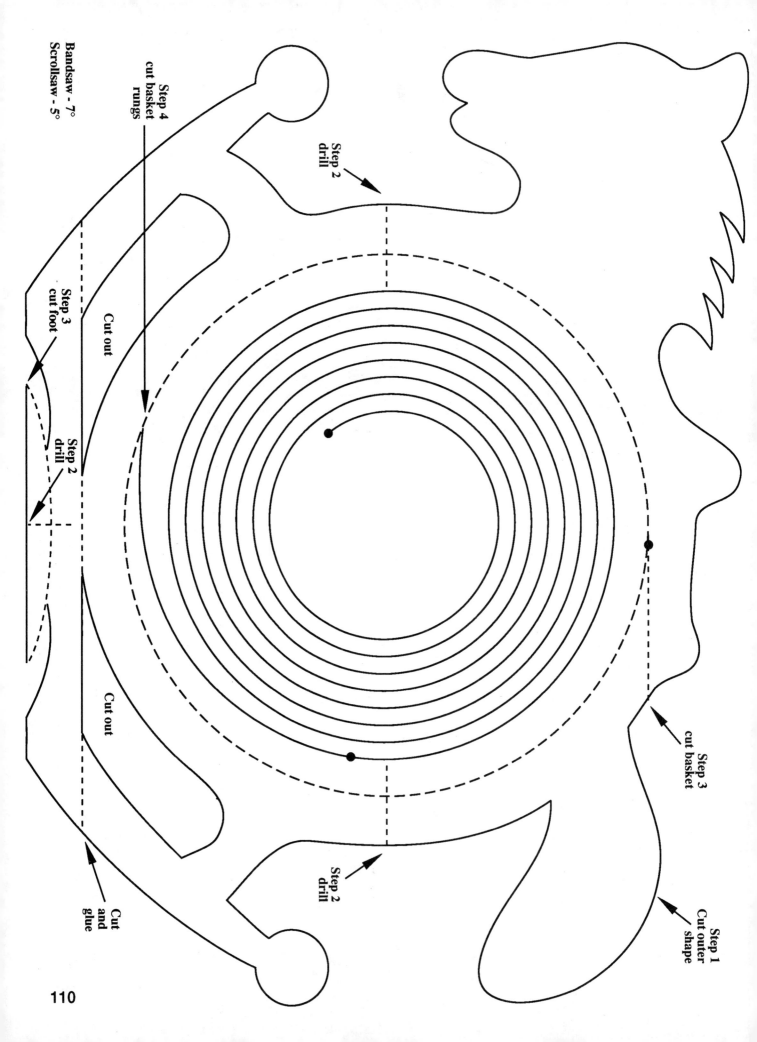

Step 2
drill

Step 4
cut basket
rungs

Bandsaw - 7°
Scrollsaw - 5°

Step 3
cut foot

Cut out

Step 2
drill

Cut out

Cut
and
glue

Step 3
cut basket

Step 1
Cut outer
shape

Step 2
drill

110

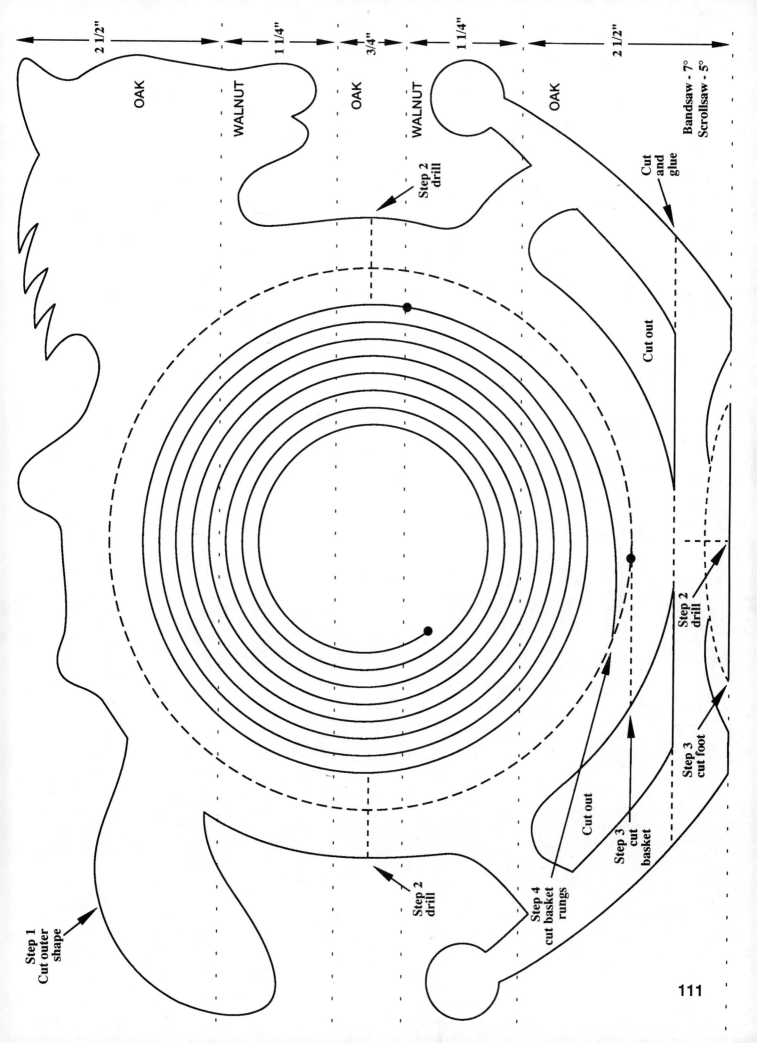

2 1/2"

OAK

1 1/4"

WALNUT

3/4"

OAK

1 1/4"

WALNUT

Step 2
drill

2 1/2"

OAK

Cut
and
glue

Bandsaw - 7°
Scrollsaw - 5°

Cut out

Step 1
Cut outer
shape

Step 2
drill

Step 2
drill

Step 4
cut basket
rungs

Cut out

Step 3
cut
basket

Step 3
cut foot

111

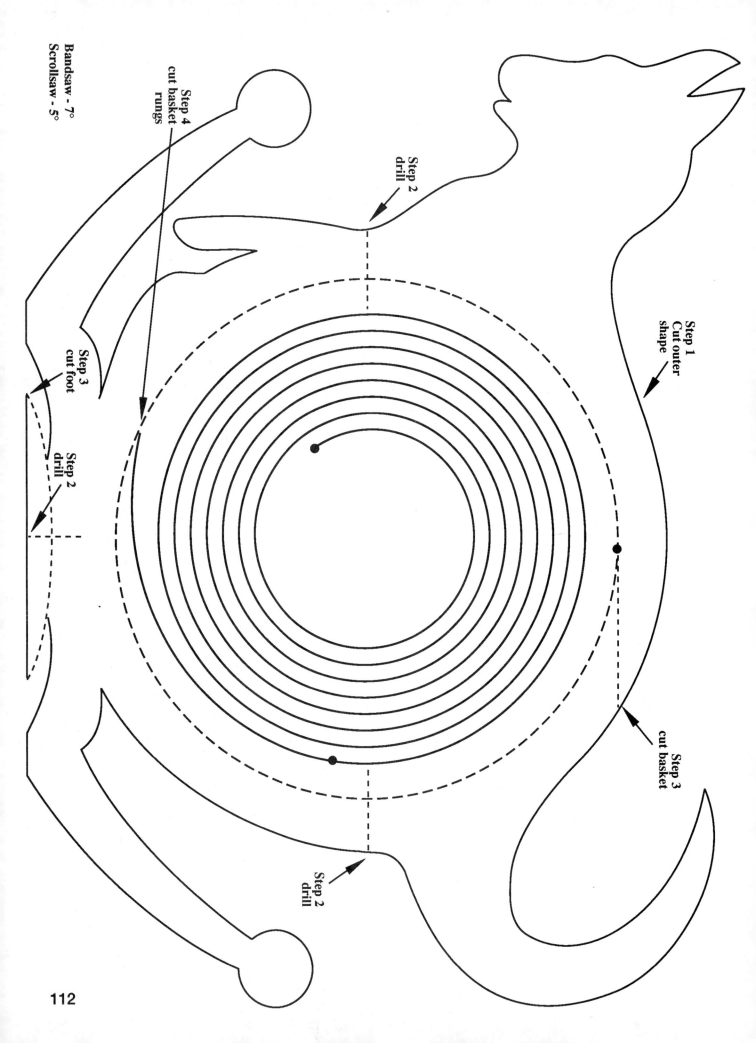

Step 4
cut basket
rungs

Step 2
drill

Step 1
Cut outer
shape

Step 3
cut foot

Step 2
drill

Step 3
cut basket

Step 2
drill

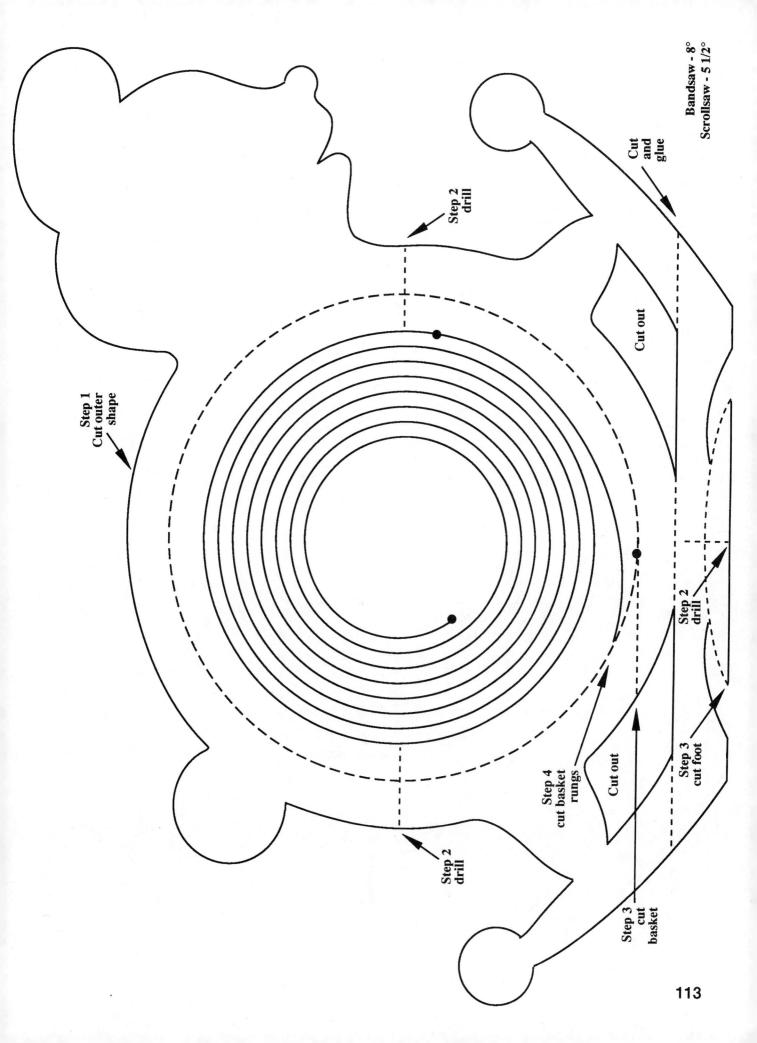

Step 2 drill

Step 1
Cut outer
shape

Cut and
glue

Bandsaw - 8°
Scrollsaw - 5 1/2°

Cut out

Step 2
drill

Step 3
cut foot

Step 4
cut basket
rungs

Cut out

Step 2
drill

Step 3
cut
basket

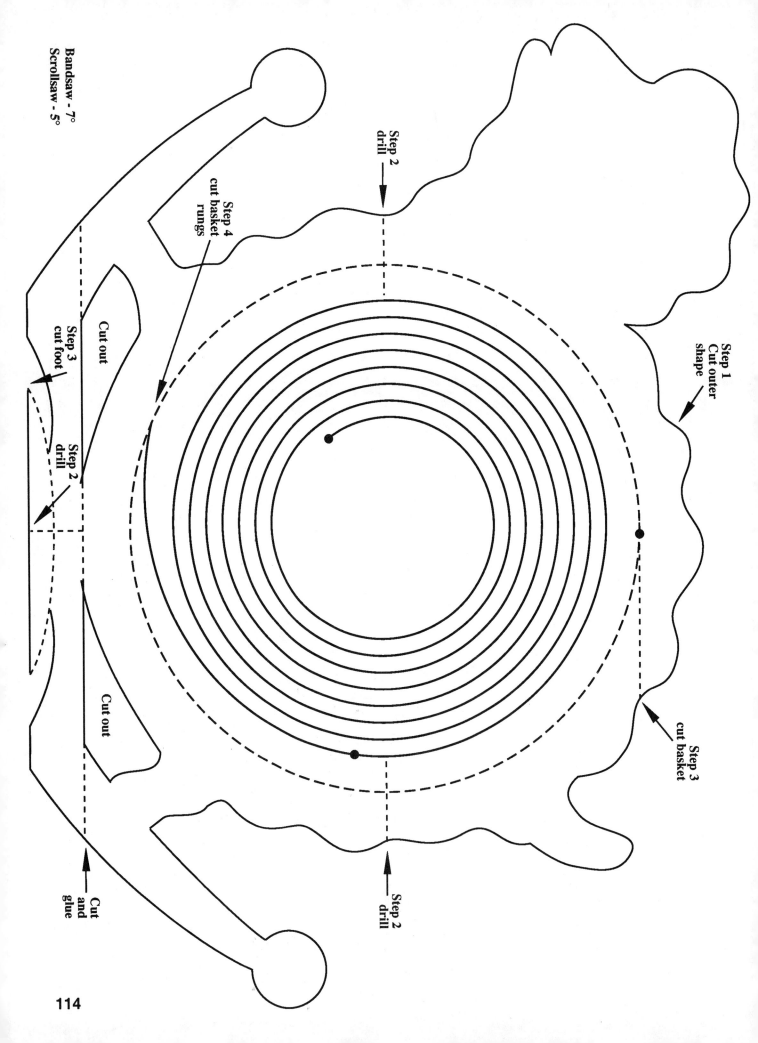

Bandsaw - 7°
Scrollsaw - 5°

Step 4
cut basket
rungs

Step 2
drill

Step 1
Cut outer
shape

Cut out

Step 3
cut foot

Step 2
drill

Step 3
cut basket

Cut out

Cut
and
glue

Step 2
drill

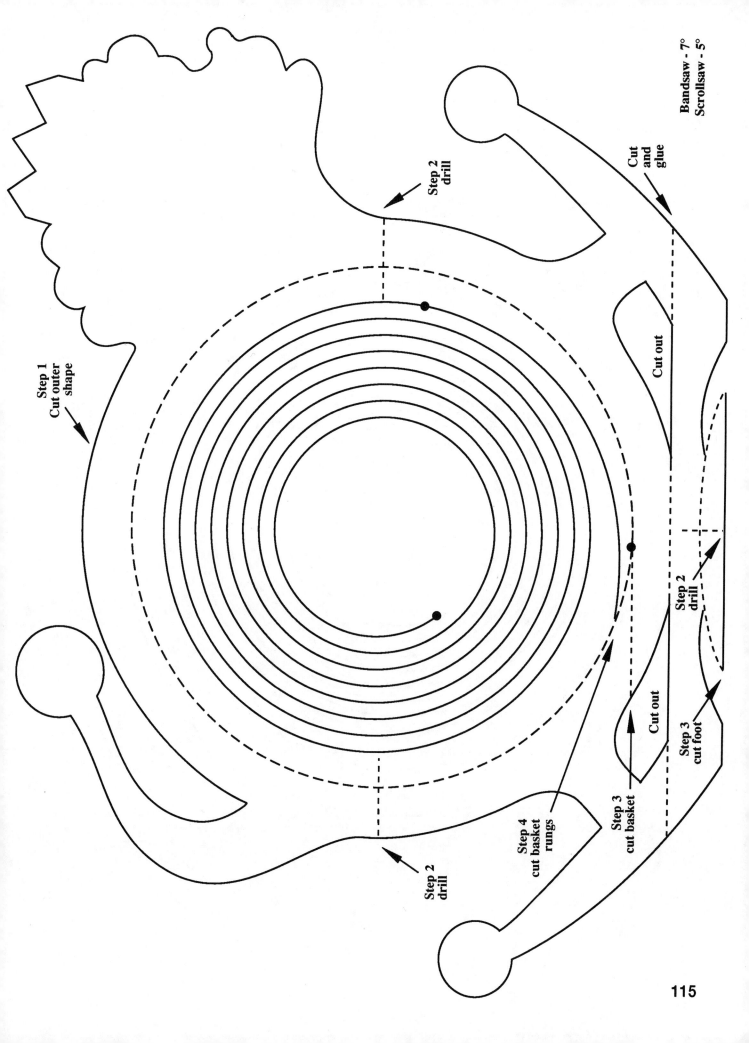

Bandsaw - 7°
Scrollsaw - 5°

Step 2
drill

Cut
and
glue

Step 1
Cut outer
shape

Cut out

Step 2
drill

Step 2
drill

Step 3
cut foot

Cut out

Step 3
cut basket

Step 4
cut basket
rungs

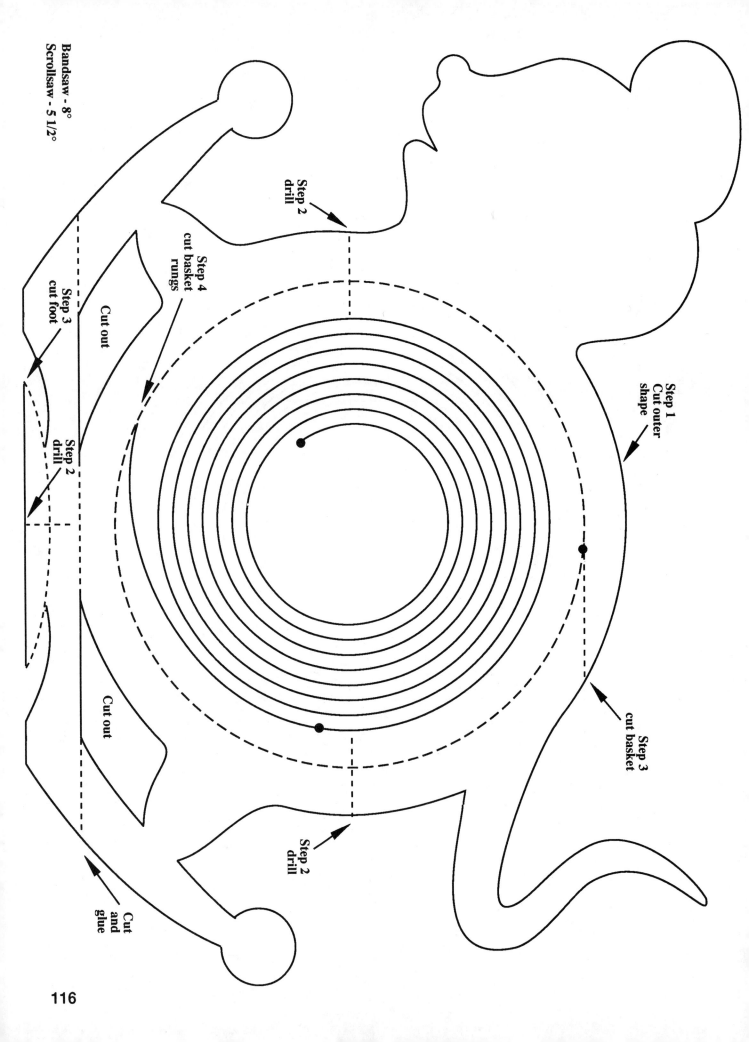

Bandsaw - 8°
Scrollsaw - 5 1/2°

Step 2
drill

Step 4
cut basket
rungs

Step 3
cut foot

Cut out

Step 2
drill

Step 1
Cut outer
shape

Step 3
cut basket

Cut out

Step 2
drill

Cut
and
glue

116

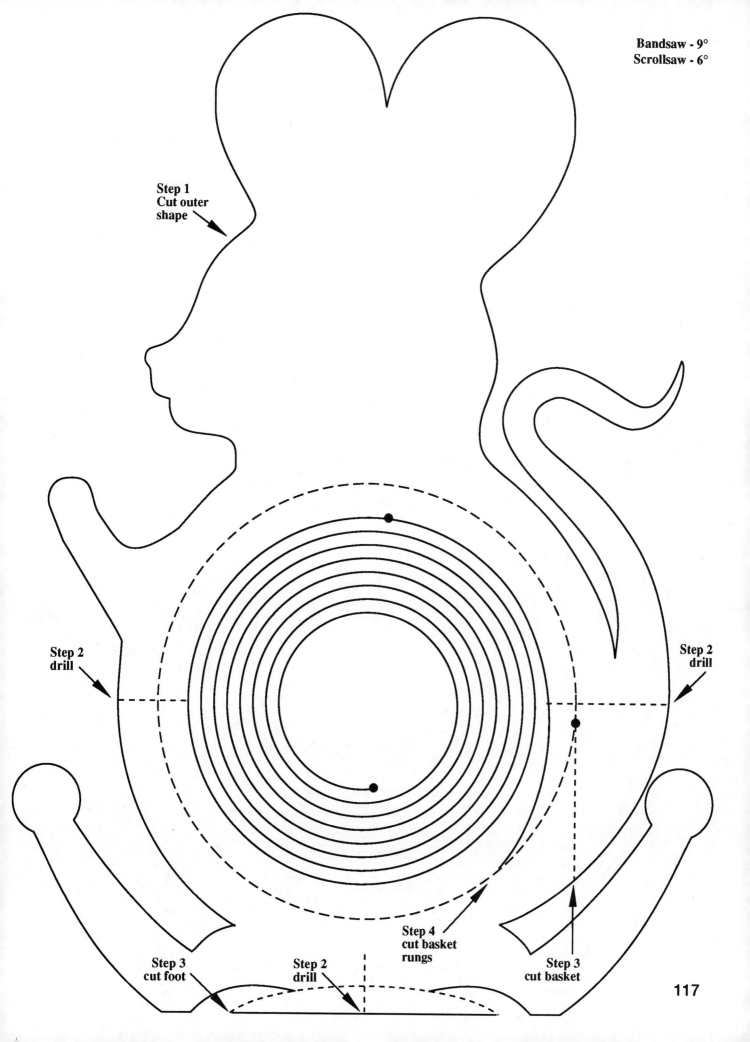

Bandsaw - 9°
Scrollsaw - 6°

Step 1
Cut outer
shape

Step 2
drill

Step 2
drill

Step 4
cut basket
rungs

Step 3
cut foot

Step 2
drill

Step 3
cut basket

117

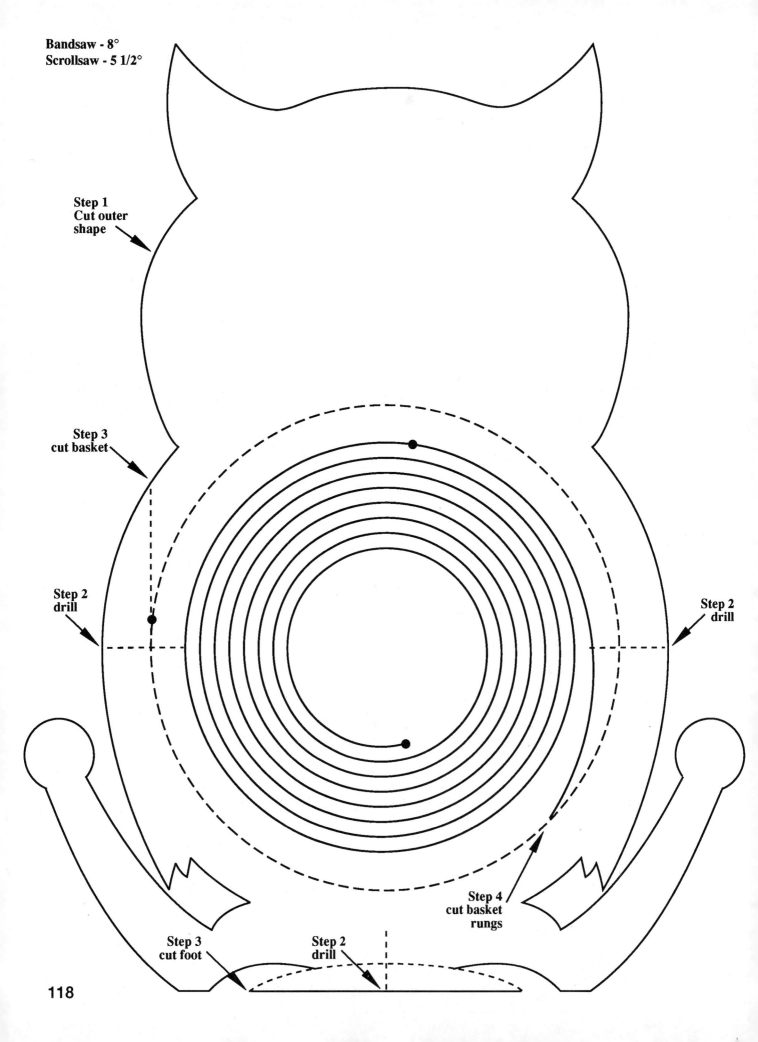

Bandsaw - 8°
Scrollsaw - 5 1/2°

Step 1
Cut outer
shape

Step 3
cut basket

Step 2
drill

Step 2
drill

Step 4
cut basket
rungs

Step 3
cut foot

Step 2
drill

118

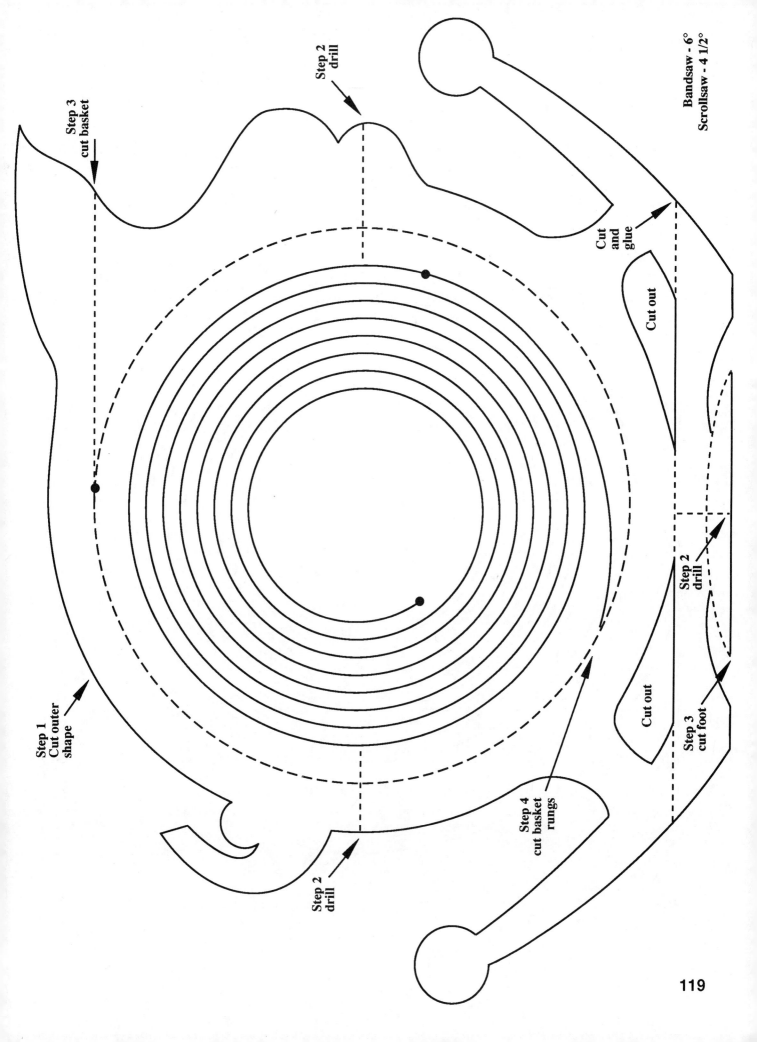

Step 3
cut basket

Step 2
drill

Bandsaw - 6°
Scrollsaw - 4 1/2°

Cut
and
glue

Cut out

Step 2
drill

Step 3
cut foot

Step 1
Cut outer
shape

Cut out

Step 4
cut basket
rungs

Step 2
drill

119

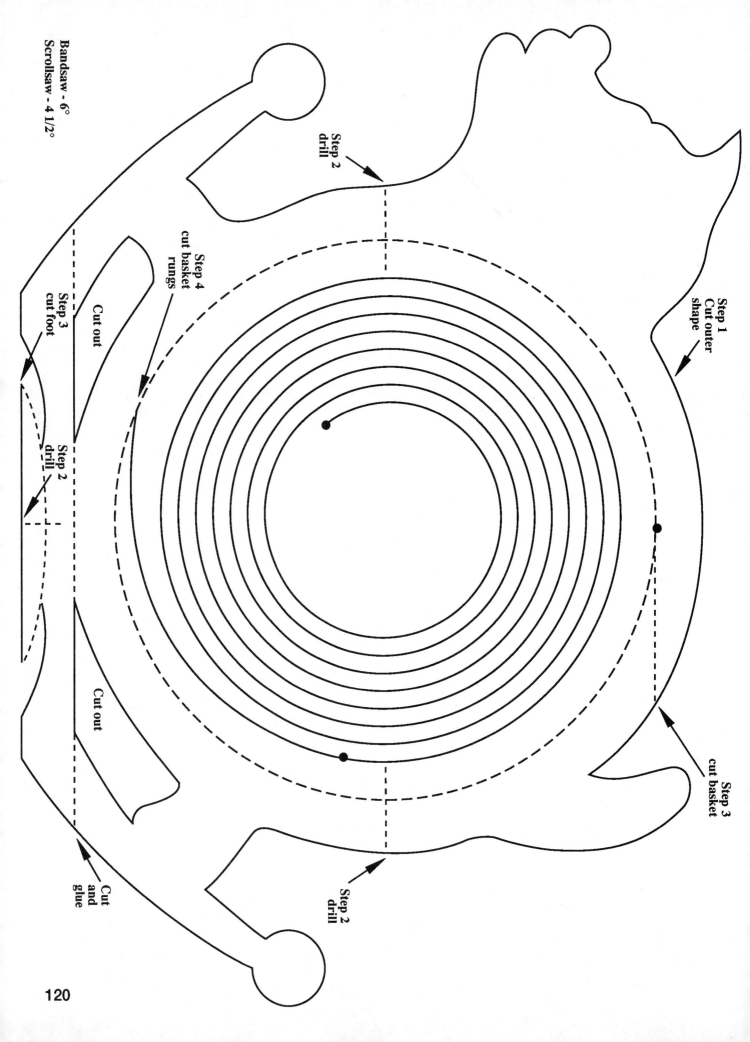

Bandsaw - 6°
Scrollsaw - 4 1/2°

Step 2
drill

Step 4
cut basket
rungs

Step 3
cut foot

Cut out

Step 2
drill

Step 1
Cut outer
shape

Cut out

Step 3
cut basket

Cut
and
glue

Step 2
drill

120

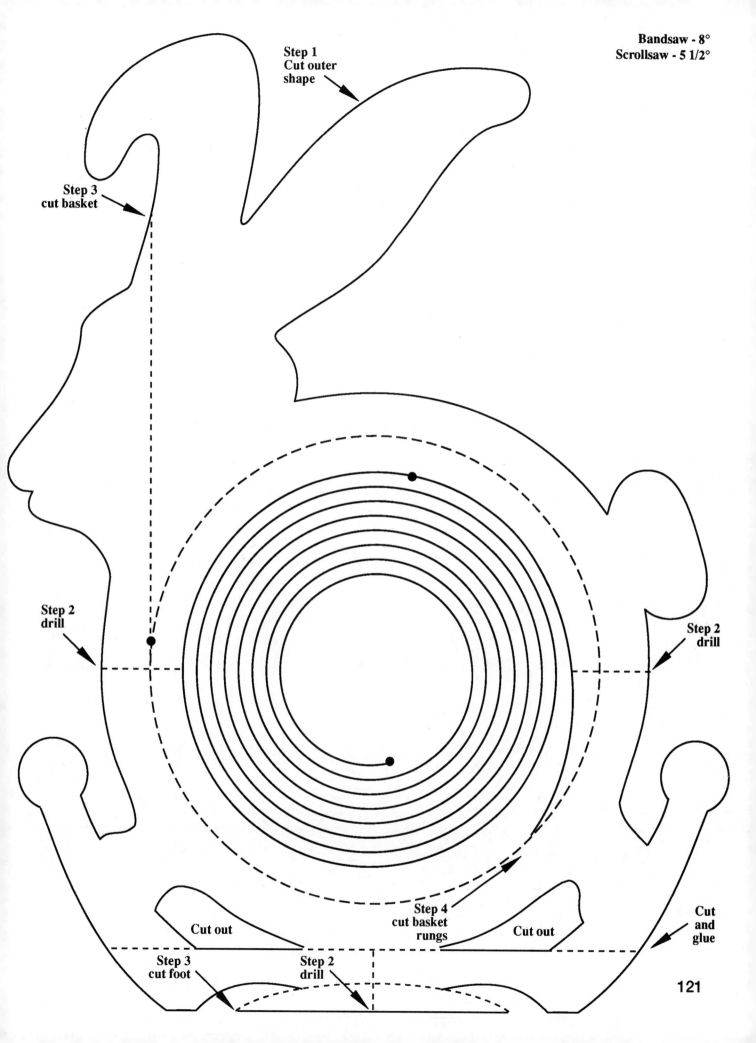

Bandsaw - 8°
Scrollsaw - 5 1/2°

Step 1
Cut outer
shape

Step 3
cut basket

Step 2
drill

Step 2
drill

Cut out

Step 4
cut basket
rungs

Cut out

Cut
and
glue

Step 3
cut foot

Step 2
drill

121

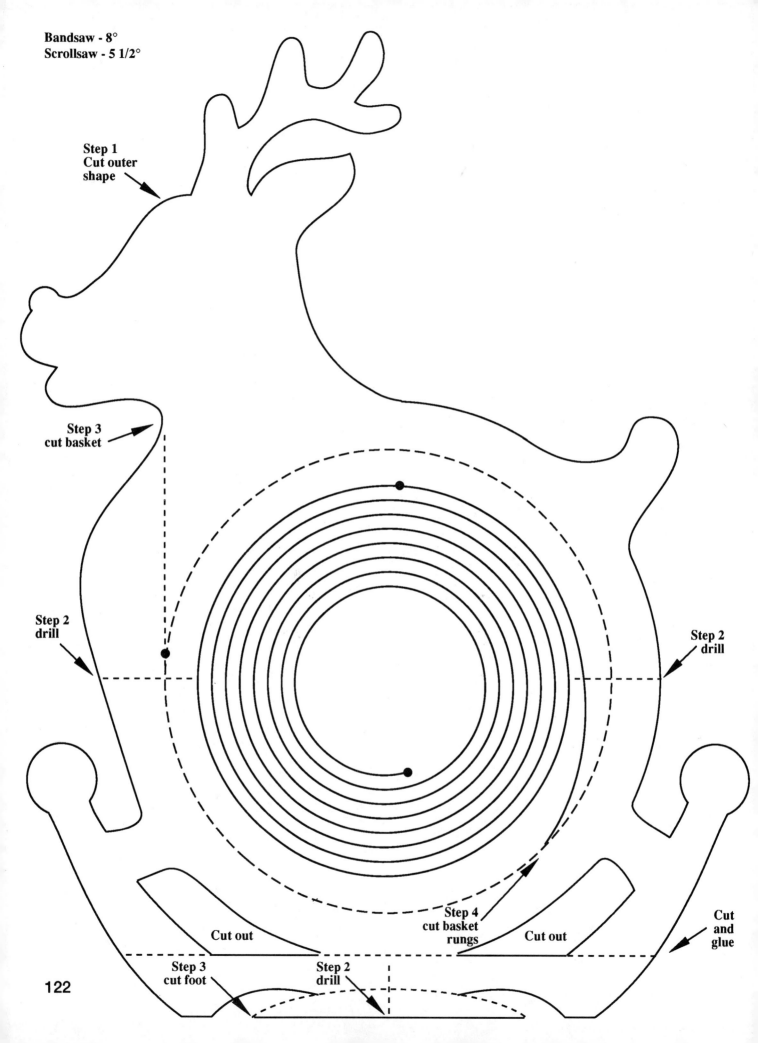

Bandsaw - 8°
Scrollsaw - 5 1/2°

Step 1
Cut outer
shape

Step 3
cut basket

Step 2
drill

Step 2
drill

Step 4
cut basket
rungs

Cut out

Cut out

Cut
and
glue

Step 3
cut foot

Step 2
drill

122

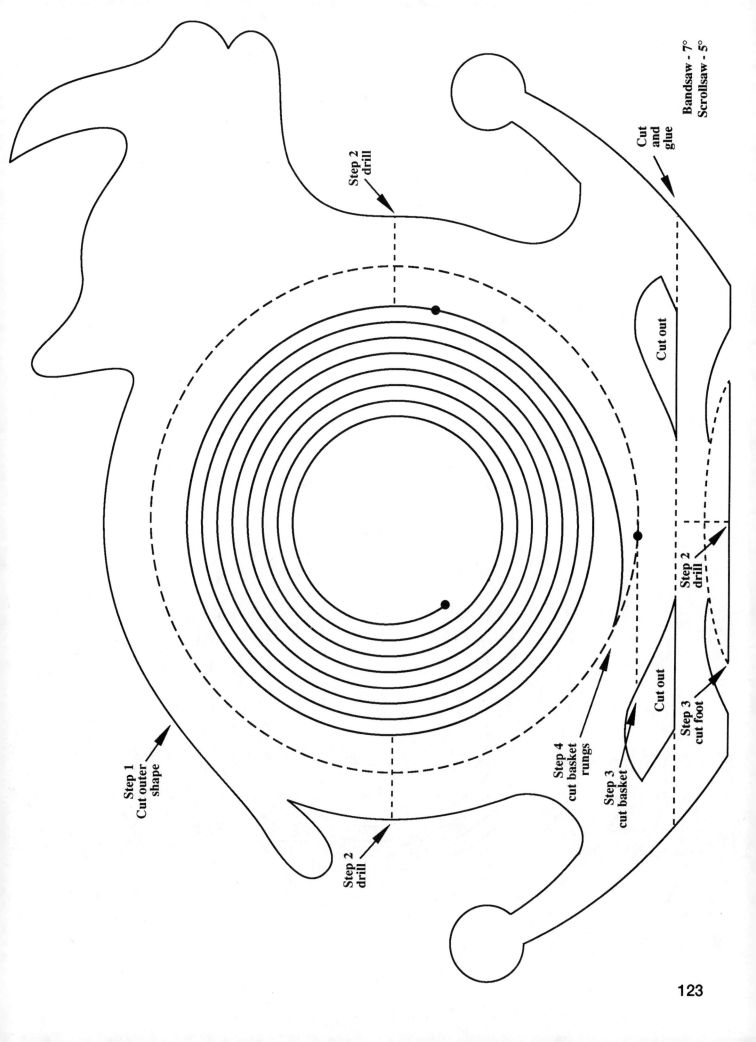

Step 2
drill

Cut
and
glue

Bandsaw - 7°
Scrollsaw - 5°

Cut out

Step 1
Cut outer
shape

Step 4
cut basket
rungs

Step 3
cut basket

Cut out

Step 2
drill

Step 3
cut foot

Step 2
drill

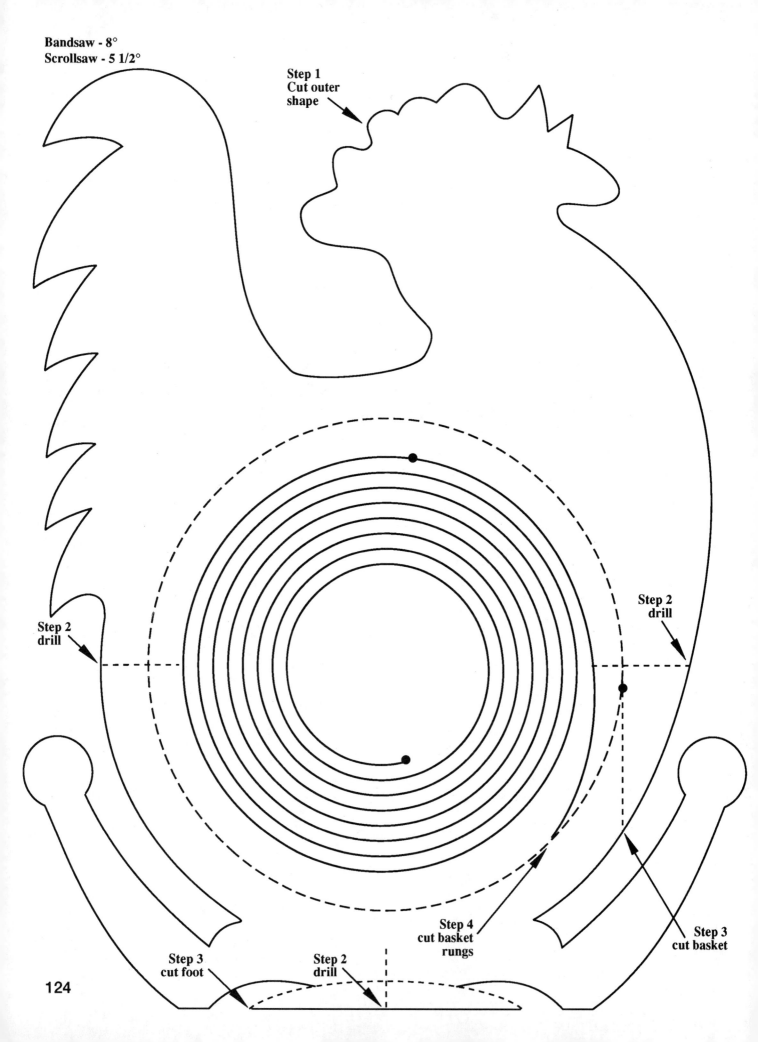

Bandsaw - 8°
Scrollsaw - 5 1/2°

**Step 1
Cut outer
shape**

**Step 2
drill**

**Step 2
drill**

**Step 2
drill**

**Step 4
cut basket
rungs**

**Step 3
cut foot**

**Step 2
drill**

**Step 3
cut basket**

124

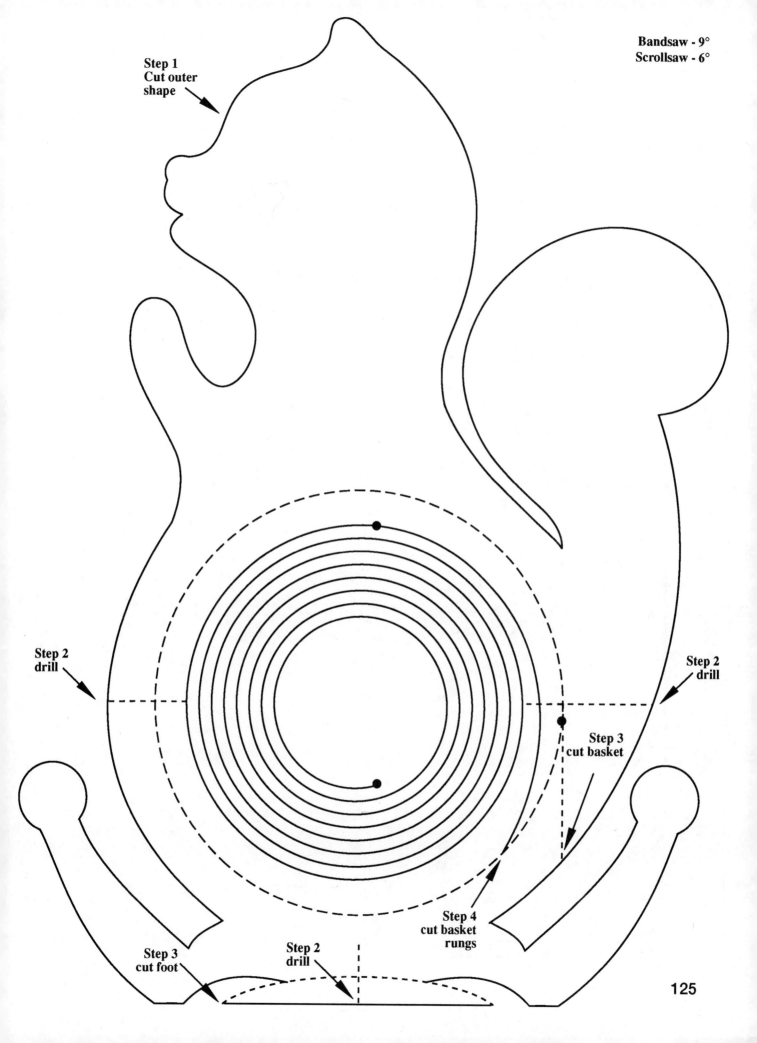

Bandsaw - 9°
Scrollsaw - 6°

Step 1
Cut outer
shape

Step 2
drill

Step 2
drill

Step 3
cut basket

Step 4
cut basket
rungs

Step 3
cut foot

Step 2
drill

125

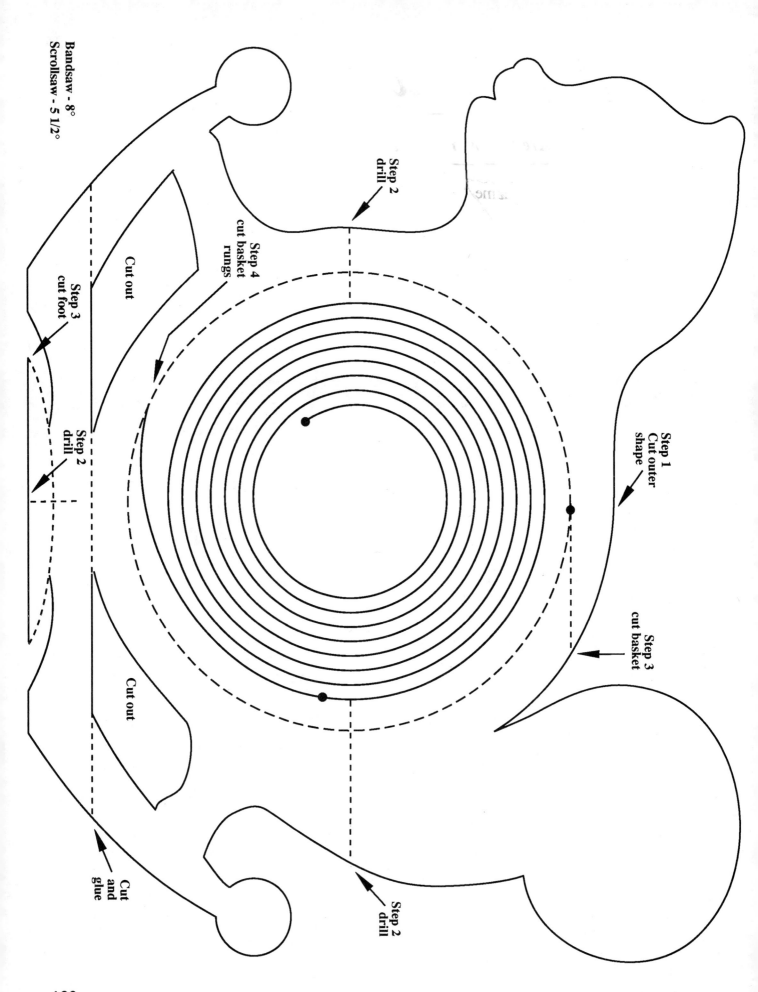

Bandsaw - 8°
Scrollsaw - 5 1/2°

Step 2
drill

Step 4
cut basket
rungs

Cut out

Step 3
cut foot

Step 2
drill

Cut out

Step 1
Cut outer
shape

Step 3
cut basket

Cut
and
glue

Step 2
drill

More Unique Designs

Are You interested in more Unique Designs ?

Yes, Please add my name to your mailing list for a catalog of more unique ideas.

Name _____

Address _____

City _____ State _____ Zip _____

THE BERRY BASKET • P.O. Box 925 • Centralia, WA 98531

BK1

Do You have Friends who are interested in a catalog of Unique Ideas ?

Yes, Please add my friend to your mailing list and send them a catalog of unique ideas.

Name _____

Address _____

City _____ State _____ Zip _____

THE BERRY BASKET • P.O. Box 925 • Centralia, WA 98531

BK1

Yes, Please add my friend to your mailing list and send them a catalog of unique ideas.

Name _____

Address _____

City _____ State _____ Zip _____

THE BERRY BASKET • P.O. Box 925 • Centralia, WA 98531

BK1

PLEASE CLIP AND MAIL